LOVING
WITHOUT
CONDITIONS

LOVING

WITHOUT

CONDITIONS

THE PATH OF CHRIST

All Glory be to God.

BENJAMIN G. BIGELOW

"Love the Lord with all your heart and with all your soul and with all your mind. This is the first and greatest commandment. And the second is like it: 'Love your neighbor as yourself'. All the Law and Prophets hang on these two commandments."

-Jesus

Truth is not a reward for good behavior. It's not given out due to a lifetime of suffering. Truth is not found more easily by the "high-minded". Truth is open and free to anyone. Truth has always been with us. Truth is found by the common person that looks where it is.

CONTENTS

PROLOGUE

Why is it that Jesus' first and most direct teaching gets so little attention? Why is it that the focus for many churches tends to be on other things—history, politics, traditions, rituals, the state of the world, finances, converting people, the end of times, etc.—without placing emphasis on the teaching of Christ before them?[1]

It would appear that the a priori condition for success in all the avenues that the church dwells in would be abidance in the Lord. That's what the teaching of Christ does. It aligns us with the patterns of Divinity, expressed through us as unconditional love. Every day we are bombarded with advertisements for having better health, making more money, losing weight, losing fat, better relationships, better lovemaking, being more attractive, looking younger, etc. Each of them holds out a "carrot" to us with the lure that they can complete us. If you've gone down that rabbit hole, you'll find the one thing they have in common is that they are all wrong. None of them complete us.

While we seek to fill a void inside ourselves, we easily become prey to the onslaught of propaganda shrouded in self-help, new

---

[1] Matthew 6:33

age, health & beauty, abundance, financial, diet movements, etc. I want to be clear from the start of this book. None of these things will get you to a state of inner completion.

If we want to feel complete, there is a path for us. It's been in front of us all along, but we didn't know to look there, perhaps because it was too obvious. Somehow it has eluded the vast majority of us. Has anyone ever told you, "Hey, look here. This is what this path means and does. This is what you're looking for"?

The problem is that it's been overlooked and its meaning washed away. It seems there have not been many takers in the relatively recent history. It seems the primary focus for most of Christendom has been on converting people to Jesus with grand promises (which are true) without really guiding them in the purpose of their life as a follower of Christ.

The path I am speaking of is ancient. It's the path that Christ taught. It began with Abraham and obeying God. It was refined through Moses in the Torah. Finally, it was perfected through John the Baptist and the man who became known as Jesus, the Christ. This path is called *Loving Without Conditions*. It is a path that is realizable in this lifetime for each of us.

Are you ready to take the journey of a lifetime? Are you willing to sacrifice temporary pleasure for long-term satisfaction and proper meaning? The focus of humanity has been upon the intellect. No matter how scientific, refined, and erudite the mind and its philosophies are, they easily become blinding.

The mind would have you usurp the patterns of peace and truth for its own ends. The mind can trick you into thinking confusion is truth. It will tell you the cloudy is clear. In obeying false idols, we bring hell onto earth. We are so short-sighted that we cannot even see the inevitable dooms we surrender to. The few voices crying in the wilderness who see the madness are then thought of as the "crazy ones". This is the difficulty of the times we are living in. We have placed false idols before God, and we are spiritually injured.

When the wisdom of our forefathers is spat upon society collapses. People, especially the young, somehow think that we get smarter as time progresses. That is obviously not true, not in the least. Throughout time, society will twist and turn down various alleyways and dead ends. Sometimes for the better, sometimes for the worse.

Thankfully, redemption can be at hand if we are willing to listen. No one has the answer, because the answer has always been with us in plain sight. It isn't a statement or doctrine. It's in you. It's in placing the Kingdom of Heaven before and above all else here on earth. But what does that even mean to a person in today's complex and technological world? It's in following the path set before us by the Master Himself, Jesus the Christ. It's not enough to know "about" this path. It needs you to show others the way. Not by pontificating but by embodying it. This path is called *Loving Without Conditions*.

Soon enough, beauty, joy, inner peace, wellbeing, abundance, and a feeling of completeness can and will arise. Realizing this truth is greater than giving 10,000 sermons about Christ. When we live "from" Christ, it is a constant sermon of hope to a suffering and desperate humanity. It takes our willingness, devotion, and dedication to realize the complete spectrum of what it means to love without conditions.

Christ taught this path out of compassion and love for each of us, for he knew it literally brings the Kingdom of Heaven out from within you.[2] The journey transforms our life into a gift for the world.

The path that Christ taught fulfills and transcends the plethora of promises the world dangles in front of you. If you take this path, you might look back and laugh at how you previously viewed the world. In traveling the path of Loving Without Conditions, one's life becomes better in amazing ways. As we are walking along, we suddenly notice we live in more abundance, we are more courageous, we are more heartfelt, and in our life, there is more harmony. Our inner life becomes deeper, more meaningful, more peaceful, joyful, loving, creative, fulfilling, fun, spontaneous, synchronistic, healed, wonder-filled, beautiful, exciting, secure and complete. This is not talked about enough in this world, the importance of Christ's teaching for us, because it is not understood en masse. It is not understood because our teachers are not taking the journey themselves. Life is fleeting. There is so much joy to be had. Let us not miss the opportunity.

The world is starving for your holiness. The world is starving for you to bring the healing spirit of Christ. God's love is eternally

---

[2] Luke 17:21

present[3] and abundant but needs our surrender to be known, felt, heard, and enacted in this world.[4] This world looks different and is transformed as our hearts and minds are melded with Christ. What could be a holier calling than to be a channel of God's peace and love, and to play witness to the beautiful and miraculous while on earth?

God is love. To know God is to know love. The intention of this work is that it may be a blessing and inspiration to the servant that feels called to know God by realizing the teachings of Christ. This world has enough "do-gooders" that know "about" Jesus, who set rules and regulations surrounding Christ. Few are those that actually seek to know Christ directly. The reason for this is that we must make room for God in our being, and most people don't want to change. This work is for the one bold enough to listen and answer the bidding of the Holy Spirit. The path is one of surrender. The writer of this work has been blessed by a lifelong journey with Christ. This work bubbles from his soul. Lord, please guide the reader in Thy ways. All glory be to Thee!

What a meaningful life we live in seeking to abide deeply in Christ! The verse, *Seek ye first the kingdom of God and his righteousness, and all things shall be added unto you*[5]*,* is pregnant with meaning. What will be added unto you is much more than

---

[3] John 1:4
[4] Matthew 9:37
[5] Matthew 6:33

could ever be imagined or described by words in a book. One could say it is akin to getting a new set of glasses. The world you see is transformed. Because you changed, everything changed. It is truly wonder-filled.

May there be as little of me as possible, Lord, in the writing of this book. And may you be glorified forever. I know that it is through Thy grace that we humans are exalted by coming to know Thee. For Thou art the Maker of life, as life doesn't raise itself. You are the Great Irreducible and the repository of Heaven... a shield in times of need. The shepherd of the sheep. Here I am for Thee, Lord... an ignorant servant in love with Thee.

It is through the personal journey and *transformation* by way of love, devotion, and surrender that the Holy Spirit is brought upon the earth. Through whom the promises of the Scriptures are realized through us.[6] *Rain down, rain down, oh Holy Spirit. Open our eyes. Bless our souls, O' Lord. In Thy holy name. Amen.*

---

[6] John Chapters 14-15

CHAPTER 1
WAKING UP

Awake, O sleeper!
And arise from the dead,
And Christ will shine on you.[7]

This life could be over for any of us in an instant. Any one of us could die today. How have you spent your life? Did you do what you were called here to do? Soon, very soon, you will meet your Maker. You will be accountable for the life you lived.[8] What mattered here for you? What do you want to be remembered and be held accountable for?

Many of us feel called to truth. We saw that the comforts of this life were fleeting. That we could live for something more meaningful, more endearing, even eternal. Our life is our gift to

---

[7] *Ephesians 5:14*
[8] *Romans 14:12, 2 Corinthians 5:10*

God, our fellow man, and ourselves. How will you use what you have left?

To choose to devote your life to the goal of Loving Without Conditions is the ultimate aspiration to achieving one's life potential and untapped greatness. The beauty of the teaching of Jesus is that it is a self-fulfilling plan. It affects every aspect of our life and enhances it. Not only are we aligning with the Laws of Divinity but we are also realizing the greatness that previously lay dormant inside us. To transform on the 'inside' changes and expands our experience on the 'outside'. Transformation undeniably involves personal revelation. However, it cannot help but touch all of humanity in the process, as the power of loving freedom in the individual is beyond the measurable domain. We are living in the wake of the transformation from those who came before us.

The author's experience is that the awareness of spiritual reality lies dormant and hidden inside until inspiration comes by grace. The account in this book is from personal experience.

In order to discern what is aligned with God and what is not, ask yourself, "Does this bring me closer to Christ?" The over-arching desire for the writer is to know, serve, and love Christ, and all that is Holy. From this walk comes the fruit of this little book. The intention is not to be academic in this endeavor, but to be clear and concise with what I have found leads to the Presence of God.

We are inspired by God Himself to pursue Him. It is a gift that is shared out of joy. Should you decide to follow this path, your life will change in wonderful and unforeseen ways. Gratitude arises due to the love felt. It is pleasant and makes life pleasant. It is filled with joy and makes life enjoyable. To get to a place of living in joy requires strict determination and resolve.

Alongside the inspiration to serve Christ, sometimes God bestows spiritual gifts. The writer has experienced these. Perhaps as a response to extreme devotion or a need in the world. The gifts happen of their own. Do not seek them. Rather, seek to be a steward of what you are to the best of your ability. Gifts serve as inspiration and proof of God's love for us, but they are not always helpful or necessary. I dedicate this work to God's love for you. *It knows no bounds.*

If you want to love without conditions it takes abundant dedication and devotion. It can be done, but it has to be a primary focus. The reward is greater than you can imagine. If you are inspired to take this path, it's likely because it is God's will for you. You can be thankful for that.

Being unconditionally loving doesn't mean being a perfect being. You might be rather silly, yet loving without conditions. All things have their place. The state of unconditional love simply means that our expression carries a greater context, a wider vision is carried by our lives. We see the innocence and lovability of those around us, including within ourselves. We tend to be present for others. We tend to be more patient. We carry the Spirit of God with us because we bow to that, our Maker. We can more readily be a catalyst for healing and a balm to this fractured world. We know that what we can't accomplish, the Spirit of God can. What greater honor could there be than in serving the Lord God

Almighty... that Whom created us and is the storehouse of all splendor.

We will have accidents, upsets, confusion, disruptions and more. However, we will see the value in peace and love over our selfish ways of being. This path means turning to God, instead of turning solely to our limited minds. When this is achieved and becomes routine, true loving without conditions is present. And this is our gift to God. Our life becomes a prayer for all creation.

Do you feel called to be holy? Then you must be willing to give everything. You must be ready to even lose everything. It is a humbling process, this path. This is the way of greatness. It is in being small, in the ego sense, that we can know the greatness of our Lord. How so? It is simply for the fact that as long as we think we know, that we are in charge, the limited aspects of the human being will be blocking the splendor of the Lord that is ennobled in the human being through the process of surrender and transformation.

The act of declaring one's commitment to loving without conditions will reprioritize everything in your life. We are no longer living for this world but for something beyond it. A way of framing the pathway differently is by using the word beauty. Beauty is synonymous with this path. To intend to see the beauty of all life is also to love without conditions. To see beauty in all of life means letting go of judgements and positions about what life is, and allowing the Holy Spirit to reveal *true vision*.

The Bible verse, "as you do unto the least of these, you do unto Me", is a statement of truth. All of life is Life. There could not be life unless it came from God. The Alpha and the Omega are not porous like a sponge. It pervades all. It is the prerequisite for life to be. And that is why intending to see the innocence and beauty in all life will reveal the holiness of life. Jesus said that loving our neighbor was as important as loving God. We may not like our neighbor's deeds, but their life is sacred to us nonetheless. Holy vision is a gift of loving without conditions. We ask God to help us, to replace our limited way of seeing.

If you only love those that love you, what credit is that to you?[9] If we want to know the Lord, we must die to self and rise in love. The Lord is everywhere. There's no place you can look or be that you will not be in His Holy Presence. I'm writing very directly to you: *the Lord is among us now.* The Lord is closer than your hands and feet. May we act accordingly.

It is in the giving up of that which stands in the way of love, namely our limited judgements and positions, that we will come closer to the Lord and offer this world the healing balm that it so desperately yearns for. *Every good and perfect gift is from above, coming down from the Father of Lights.*[10]

Here's the trick to loving unconditionally. It's not in the *doing.* It's not in the *trying* even. That route is slow and can be very baffling. Instead, we allow love to arise naturally by getting out of

---

[9] Luke 6:32
[10] James 1:17

the way. Remember, if we paint over rust, the rust will win out sooner or later. Changing the exterior is temporary and not a change of being necessarily. Look to the blocks to love that you carry, that's the fast route. *Love is already always present.* We don't have to try and create love. We will discuss the "how to" for removing the obstacles to the state of being called love as part of this book. When this process begins for you, it will take some diligence. Eventually, it will become a way of being. Love perfects itself. It wants to strive and grow and bless. At that point, the purpose that Christ gave us is close at hand. We want to be prepared to die well. Let us get to work today. Let us set the intention to serve the Lord.

Life took a completely different turn when I found this path. The inspiration came by grace. For some, it comes after a period of suffering. For me, it seemed to come out of nowhere. Typically, we won't choose to change or to surrender to something "higher" of our own will. My life prior, upon looking back, seemed like I was sleepwalking. But with this path, a whole new dimension opened. Many changes took place. I was not considered very creative prior, and that changed. I became more animated as a person. I was happier. I even became a smarter student; the way my brain functioned was different. I've since written over a thousand songs, whereas I struggled to write a single song before. Music has been a healing boon to my walk with God, allowing my heart to express itself through the innocence of art.

This path has brought tremendous meaning to my daily existence. Life is new every day and each day brings fulfillment. Every day is motivated and supported by love. This love has no end. Those of us who follow Christ are inspired to love and to perfect that love. Thank you God for the inspiration to surrender this life and to serve Thee in love.

Are you ready to take a journey that can open doors you never knew existed? Do you feel a subtle voice within that beckons you on to something great? I've written this book for you. It would seem there are others who feel called to know life at a greater depth, or that want to wholeheartedly surrender to the Lord, to be His servant.

People in your life may resent you for choosing this path. Many may be skeptical. Most in my life have not understood. Most of the Christians in my life might go to church and will say Jesus is their savior, but are not inspired to live for Him. Greater than our verbal belief in God is the way people live their life. That speaks the truth of what they really believe and who they really are.

In general, the majority of people are driven by succeeding in the material matters of the world; having more and looking great. We cannot blame anyone for this, we are all doing our best. For this path, we must drop our need for approval, even from other Christians. We must remember that even Christ Jesus was not accepted. He was misunderstood and shunned by most. He also warns us that the same will happen to us who follow His calling.

A few things are certain: You are worthy of the journey because you exist. You don't need anyone's permission. The door is open. You are worthy because you are part of Creation. You are loved because that is the truth of life. You will learn to forgive the thoughts that hold you as anything lesser while being humble enough to respect your limitations in this world.

If I have learned anything from a life devoted to the Lord, it is this: God loves us more than we can imagine.[11] If it's true for one, it's true for all. As we etch away the stagnation keeping us from knowing pure love and the mystical states that are waiting for us, we come to see a clearer picture of God's love for all of life. God's love is always 100% present. God is always with open arms. No one is forced to choose for God, but it is the most logical and wise choice on our part that we could ever make.

Choosing for God doesn't mean smooth sailing from that point onward. There are parts of us that will change. Since we tend to resist change, this can spurn some difficulty and struggle. The way through this: *Surrendering our will to God's Will.* As we learn to surrender, we flow *with* life, instead of *against* life.

Unaided, the mind will project human limitations onto God. It's hard for us to imagine something outside of the box of our perceived view of reality and what life is, but the realm of God is of a totally different paradigm than our limited existence. We can only ever get a glimpse of this, by Grace. But the more deeply we

---

[11] Luke 12:32

delve into this path, the more deeply we will come to know the Father's love as simply being indescribable and miraculous, yet always present.

Our experience from childhood tends to be projected onto God as a father. Instead of allowing God to reveal Himself to us, we perceive Him through a filter of limitations. We can open our hearts and mind to the Lord, and come to Him empty-handed. Do yourself a favor and trust in the mercy of the Lord and His Will for you. It is all one could ever ask for. Through this, you will know and do amazing things. Jesus says that "it's the Father's good *pleasure* to give you the Kingdom." Our act of love and service is also to receive this love fully. Our obedience is to the Source of love. I dedicate this work to God, who is our Rock, our Source, our Sustenance, our Savior, our Redeemer... the Presence that is with you now. Be our eyes oh Lord. Let us be used by Thy Sacred and Beautiful Eyes.

CHAPTER 2
LOVING WITHOUT CONDITIONS

My Command is this: Love each other
as I have loved you.[12]

This is the task at hand: *to love without conditions*. This is the aim that fuels and guides our life. It aligns everything we do. We are a different person because of this intention, and life interacts with us differently. Our life is filled with meaning, hope, goodwill, and increasing humility and joy. Don't give in to doubt! Rise up and walk. Every journey starts with a single step.

There is no greater honor in life than to receive this quest for your life. It means that Grace already has Her hand upon you. Don't take this for granted! Many are they that have once been inspired only to fall into the snares of complacency and the irrelevant. Treat this like a fire that life depends upon. It's raining

---

[12] John 15:12

outside, you're hungry, and life depends upon keeping this fire. That's the passion to enlist from within. You must treat it with care. You must get down on your knees. Cup your hands around this fire and shield it from the wind. Help it along so it can become a beautiful blazing fire that lights up your life.

We hear so much about love in this world. What is it? Firstly, most of how love is expressed in popular culture, via all forms of media, really stems from desire, control, and gain. It's a tradeoff type "love," which is not love at all. It's temporary possession and evanescent. "You make me feel so high, you make me feel so good..." This has nothing to do with what we are talking about on this path.

Love is readily acknowledged in our culture with a parent's love for their child, love between war veterans, teammates in sports, and love for pets. These forms of love are accepted en masse and understood by most.

The love that we are speaking about in this book is an inner radiance. *A way of being.* It's not in the specifics, it's not controlled. It's not in the trying. It's a state of being that we surrender to. The actions that stem from this way of being are lovingness, sweetness, uplifting, caringness, concern, being present, strength, stillness, life enhancing, and bravery. It uplifts others in seeming subtle but powerful ways. It holds the door for others regardless of the social milieu of the day. It sacrifices itself for others. The parent makes breakfast for their child every morning and delights to see them eat it. They're aware that the child takes this service for granted. That doesn't matter. We fill up the gas tank when we borrow our partner's car so that they won't be inconvenienced. We can keep our house clean and in order out of love for others that live in it. We know their life will be all the better for it. We wipe the dirty hand print off the refrigerator door because we want the room to look beautiful. We might not formally recognize it, but it is love. We slow down the car when driving so the person a block ahead does not have to feel rushed when crossing the street. We complement the beauty in others and reflect it back to them. Love says: *your life, experience and wellbeing mean something to me. In fact, they are as important to me as my own life and wellbeing.* Love wants nothing in return. The act of true love is sufficient and is satisfied being what it is.

People that come from love as a way of being aren't loving particulars about another. They are loving the *whole* of 'others.' Love makes us feel "at one" with another. Ultimately, we find that Jesus is loving through us, and this results in the loving of souls, the part that is eternal. The "life" of a being. The soul is validated, upheld, and revered in true lovingness. We leave behind all programs and meet as children.

We do things from the spirit of love for the sake of love, and that love is ultimately always for God. It is the Grace of God beckoning us and returning us to God Himself, the Source of all life. We do not look for rewards; enough is the act of love and the joy that emanates from it. We let go of the codependent aspects of love, people-pleasing and wanting approval. We instead live from our heart and the unseen hum of the Presence of God that reveals itself solely to the loving and selfless.

__Greater love hath no man than this, that he lay down his life for his friends.__ [13]

Laying down our life for others could potentially mean the act of physically using our body to protect others. However, more aptly, it means letting go of resistance, attachment to limiting judgements, fears, and negative thinking. This is how we become truly loving. It is when blocks to love are let go that the true light of joy shines and blesses those around us. This light is always available, but we had chosen other options out of habit and literally missed the light. In fact, the light just is. No one and nothing can change that.

The realm of suffering happens because we have created a separate identity away from God. We fell from grace. We are no longer walking in the garden. The way back is to realize that the world we have made up in our minds is fictious. So then, it is safe to let go of whatever is not of love, peace, and truth. With devotion and dedication to loving without conditions, we see moments of resistance and inner stagnation as an opportunity. We become willing to do the work. It is not an overnight process but a transformation in how we view our life that leads to a better quality of living. We will go into the mechanics of letting go in another part of this book. This process becomes a habit and is a key that springs us into the realm of everyday joy.

---

[13] John 15:13

I see many Christians focused on history, proving Jesus' genealogy, debating what Jesus actually meant, taking pride in having defined the Christian experience for everyone, debating about what sect is most Christian, the problems with the 'other' sects, synchronistic numbers in the bible, worshipping a book in a black and white way of thinking, fear-based interpretations, end of times predictions, etc., *while not focusing on where Jesus actually is to be found.* Those things are more or less diversions. Jesus will not be found in the past. A life with Jesus isn't even about going to church. Going to church may be a boost to your spiritual propensities through devotion, but if we are to have a meaningful relationship with Jesus, it starts now. It's something real and profound. It changes everything about us. It's alive, it's full, and it gives much more than this world can ever offer on its best days.

If we are to use the Bible to find Jesus, it must point us to where he is to be found. The place we find and have a relationship with Jesus is in our hearts. Your relationship with God does not depend on mental gymnastics or trying to prove anything about God. It only depends on you, Jesus, and your openness to Him. You're inviting Him into your heart[14] to live with you and through you. *This relationship with Jesus is the catalyst that changes the world.* Most of the world is in spiritual depravity and suffering. This relationship, when we are spiritually devoted to it, is itself the wellspring of spiritual abundance. Through this relationship comes a change in the filter through which one sees the world. Our thinking changes. What seemed real before is now different. What

---

[14] Romans 2:14-15

is unproductive and not beneficial in life will readily slip away as we align with God.

We have only so much time and energy on this plane. If how we are living our faith is based on faulty assumptions, we can labor in vain. People argue the faith and try to prove its truth via the level of reason. You can almost feel them grab your arm when they tell you what they believe is the "right way". This is the world of form, which itself is limited and chaotic. We must live for something greater than form. God is not grading you. God does not have human limitations. He is, by nature, unlimited. If people ask for an opinion, I tend to give it saying, "this is how it appears to me," knowing full well that I am just one experience and that this could change. How you live your life speaks more about you than your words about your faith or the meaning of life.

When there is force involved in our proselytizing we often end up pushing others away. To preach Jesus in this way can lead to shutting the doors of heaven in front of others. If we want to open the doors of heaven for others, we must come from heaven to do so.

It is a good thing to defend the faith. However, that argument must be done with humility and love, in an inviting way. One typically does not find God through logic. Logic and reason cannot encompass or encapsulate God. True evangelizing comes through the power of our relationship with God and is sanctified by the Holy Spirit. If you love Jesus, you are His spokesperson on earth according to others that don't know Him already. If you are his spokesperson, wouldn't you want the fruits of that relationship to be sweet, ripe, and pure for the suffering souls to encounter in this world? Indeed, of course we do. Let us shine with the light of love and thanksgiving.

The greatest proselytizing we will ever do is living a holy and joy-filled life. What is odd is that Jesus has taught about the Pharisees and the scribes and those who thought they had the market cornered on God. They had memorized the scriptures and felt they were morally superior to others because of this. They were teachers and scholars that felt they did the "right things" for God. Jesus saw through them. Jesus saw them as he sees us. He saw to their hearts. Jesus is not fooled by outward appearances. That which is not of love is not of love. That which is not sanctified by the Holy Spirit does not come from God. Pride makes one blind. Humility opens up and invites God in. The Pharisees and scribes were stuck in the vanity of "knowing about". Do not be like the Pharisees and think you are the "right one" while everyone else is "wrong". If we go to a bible study, there is often no shortage of Pharisees. To know God, we must see our personal limitations and abilities.

Speaking about what we "know" is different from speaking about what we "know about." Speaking from what you know has integrity. I felt inspired years ago to become a pastor, to write books, or to do something in the world of religion and spirituality. I luckily decided I wouldn't share about God until it no longer mattered to me to do so. Not until I felt complete and stopped wanting to change others "for their own good." Now, I share from a place of being. I share fully realizing this is just one experience of one soul. This is who I am. I stand naked before God. Take it or leave it. That's not in my control. God's will be done.

God's word must be written in our hearts.[15] It needs no defense. The only way to transform anyone is by first transforming one's own life through the Word and Will of God. This likely cannot be done without deconstruction of who we think we are and what life is. Transformation can bring about much change. The false will eventually fall away. We cannot advance spiritually without honest adherence to God.

We must be careful with strong political judgments and opinions, as those can set us up for falling into the vanity of pride. "Render unto Caesar what is Caesar's, and unto God what is God's." There is the path of loving without conditions, then there is the path of the political enthusiast. They are two different callings that lead to different destinations. One leads to being embroiled in the clatter for which there is no ultimate answer. The other is a different calling, leading to a life of joyful servitude that glorifies life by a shining, inner radiance.

We can see the limitations of all thought systems. Not any single one has all the answers. Each sees a certain part and mostly excludes what they can't see. We can have compassion on even our own views because we realize them as limited. It's ok to have an opinion, but we do not need to be "right." We do not have to have all the answers. Jesus Christ has His role, and we have ours. We are not omniscient, and so even our own mind's ideas become a "this seems to be true at present, until further evidence is shown."

---

[15] Psalm 40:8

With this attitude, we feel more free and easy going. It makes it easier for others to be around us. And we can more easily avoid the chagrin of our prideful blunders.

Greatness is there for you. Can you see it? Wake up. We are the poor banished children of Eden. You are walking in a temporary space suit; the body. This will all be over in a flash. Yet, your greatness is always outside of time. It's your inheritance by default. Say "yes" to your greatness. It's what Christ wants. Greatness doesn't come from succumbing to the detractors of the human spirit. Break free from being a slave to lust, anger, apathy, ignorance or the one million other forms of littleness keeping one in the dream of nothingness. Come out of hiding. It is safe. There is no other way. We will not find rest until we do. Stop sitting on your laurels. God loves you. God is unlimited opportunity. You are free to receive this opportunity now.

What do all the words mean in this book mean? It means the cage of unnecessary suffering we are engrossed in is of our own creation. At some point, we said "yes" to the energy fields and thought patterns of limitation that present themselves to the mind. At some point, fear arose, and we accepted it by saying "yes" to it, rather than seeing through it and choosing for our greatness. How is this choice undone? *Christ already un-chose it for you.* However, His sacrifice comes to fruition only when we say *"yes"* to our greatness. That greatness is dormant until enacted by your noble choice. Be blessed my friend. Own your greatness. Your life is building a large castle, whether you like it or not. Brick by brick, stone by stone... You can stay complacent in the dungeons, or you can go upstairs and see the magnificent views. Sure, there are stairs to climb. Do not think about how many, that is fruitless. Simply take the next step. That is it!

The world where Christ won our salvation may be unseen to you at present. But it will open up to you, in it's own way and time, in the exact amount that you choose *for* it. You will realize it was what you always dreamed of and wanted. It was there in the back of your mind, but you were sleeping. Your deepest dreams come true here. It's hard to verbalize, but it is the truth. There is a hand reaching out to you; I can only hope you choose for your greatness because I love you with the love of Christ.

CHAPTER 3
DEVOTION AND WILLINGNESS

Ask, and it will be given to you.
Seek, and you will find.
Knock, and it will be opened unto you.[16]

How do we approach the idea of *Loving Without Conditions*? How is this idea achieved? There are two important factors at our disposal: **devotion** and **willingness**. These two go hand in hand, and without them, nothing is accomplished.

Of course we rely on perception for physical survival. This has been ingrained in us since before we started walking. However, our perception is prone to error, prone to selfishness, prone to littleness, and therefore limited judgement. Because of this our experience is limited. We continually shut the door to the Kingdom of Heaven for ourselves and, by default, others in the

---

[16] Matthew 7:7

process. This might come as a shock, but if you're not living in extreme joy in this moment, you are shutting the door to heaven with your limited perception. This is why Jesus beckons us to forgive and to love. In this pursuit, the kingdom of heaven is revealed. We are called to stand up and choose what matters: to bring the presence of Peace to a suffering world. To do so is to be Christ's servants and help fulfill his mission on earth.

It had long been held that surpassing the 4-minute mile was impossible for humans. A man named Roger Bannister broke through that barrier and showed the world it was possible. Because of his belief, his devotion to the task, and his willingness to try, he created a new paradigm for all runners. This task, which no one had ever done before, was surpassed again within 46 days of his accomplishment. Human beings as a species didn't physically change in those 46 days, only their belief in what was possible changed. There was a paradigm shift for runners of the time.

We are living within and potentially creating new paradigms with our life. If you're asleep, you're more than likely trailing in the wake of others, unbeknownst to you. Much like a leaf that has landed in a stream. However, if you're reading a book such as this, it's likely you've been touched and are in the process of awakening.

What will you do with your life? Will you reveal to humanity the endless possibilities of love and a relationship with Christ? Will you help save the souls of others? This world has enough "do-gooders." It has enough people talking about love. It has so few that actually submit to love. Will you follow? Will you create? Will you open the way for the untold others, leaving your mark on this world?

Devotion is a balm to the body, mind and spirit. It is the means by which we are in continuous communication with the Lord. Devotion is always available. It is our birthright, the ability to open directly to that whom created us.

It is through our devotion that all avenues of holiness and beauty open to us. Devotion is a positive act of surrender. It's saying, "Lord, I am here for You. Come, take my life. Do with me according to Thy Will. How would you have me?" Devotion is love inspired. Devotion is what makes the impossible possible, transforming life from the mundane into the beauty all around us. Devotion is the precursor to the miraculous.

Devotion gives life deep and profound meaning. It is the meaning of life that we seek so much, whether we know it or not, to help give purpose to a life filled with suffering and toil. Life changes. Devotion is directed towards that which does not change. The changeless reveals itself to the devoted.

The devoted are not always understood. When you are passionate and devoted to something, you go into the subject deeply. When you live for love, it will separate you in more ways than you thought possible. Most of the world is programmed to 'get', 'achieve', 'acquire' and 'amass'. However, this is not the path of holiness. In the path of holiness, we die to ourselves and the world. We become small in world desires. Fame, money, sexual attraction, etc., are seen to be limited and potential traps that can keep us from where we want to be. But let it be known, though the path is humbling, it is a strong fortress in this life and the next.[17] We may sacrifice temporary pleasures and avoid their temptations along the way so that our sacrifice pays dividends in love.[18] It is this power, which we must call love, that changes the world from within. Nothing and no one can stop it. Not only is it important to the continuance of humanity, but it also turns the human experience into a great school for the Christian. And how great is the reward!

Willingness is the fuel to nearly all worthy human endeavors. We find the willingness to go into places we would normally resist in order to realize our goal. Devotion fuels willingness, and willingness is the backbone of devotion. "All for Thee, oh Lord!" is the mantra that aligns the life of the devoted. We are able to love without condition because we come to see that what matters is that which is Eternal. We start to tune into the Presence of the Almighty more, which works as a compass in our daily life. We may start to have profound experiences as well, and these only

---

[17] See the 'Sermon on the Mount'
[18] Matthew 6:19-20

further our passion to join with and know our God of love all the more.

Often times on this path we are beset with temporary but incredible pain. That's because in order for our hearts to open, sometimes they need to be cracked a little bit. Some of us more than others. If there is hardness there, how can the Presence of the Lord enter? Therefore, start making a soft and welcoming domain for the Lord to enter. He's awaiting your entreaty! Your willingness to say "yes" will bring it about. You are investing in yourself, and there is no greater investment that you could do for your life.

There can also be pain when we discover that we've withheld love from ourselves and the world. This can be both in the present or from the past. Since we are looking at the world differently, some of the things we do or have done are no longer acceptable. Our mistakes can rise up suddenly and take us by surprise. Sometimes guilt or shame will accompany this realization. It is important to have compassion for oneself and realize this is actually a step forward. This is part of growth. The process of change is not easy for any creation. But it is inevitable. Your willingness to say "yes" to what comes and to see it through will be the process of how you earn your wisdom. Wisdom is the hard-fought-for gift of life.

A friend asked me recently if I felt that I had used this life wisely. If I felt that I was utilizing my gifts. Because of the intention to be loving without conditions and for the desire to be a servant of the Lord, it was easy for me to say "yes." I cannot judge my life. I can only look to my intention. There is no path more fulfilling and nourishing than to be on the path of unconditional love.

Because the overarching goal of each day is to be used as a channel of love, every day has tremendous meaning. Difficult days are an opportunity to love. Days filled with joy and ease are opportunities to glorify the Lord and enjoy His bounty.

Happiness in the world is fleeting and depends on conditions, which are never stable. The only thing that does not change is God. No matter the appearance, it is safe to have complete faith in the love of God and to surrender your will to Him.

Your best friend is *Jesus*, whether you have realized this or not. Jesus is the greatest gift the world has ever known. One is free to doubt this. Normally, this is revealed by the Holy Spirit to a person, and it transforms them forever. Never in the history of people has this phenomenon, known as Jesus, been born to ignorant and unaware people. One with the Father. Completely divine. He came as a living sacrifice for all. But why? Because most of us are bogged down by the weight of our ignorance. He came as a protector, to save people from themselves. It is by our own end that we know hell. The radiance of Jesus transcends all time. It is because of His grace that this book is written, without which this work could not happen.

Resistance to seeing the beauty of Jesus is normally simply resistance to love. Jesus is love, the epitome of love. What is there to not like? It is holding onto concepts of what Jesus Christ is *not* that causes confusion and shows Jesus in any other light than absolute love.

Many times people will mistake Christians for Christ. Christians are just people like everyone else that are (hopefully) trying to be Christ-like. One doesn't have to buy into the religion, per se, to love Jesus. Christianity is made up of humans. Humans tend to err. Christians that strive to realize His teachings are bright lights amongst lights here on earth. Through humility, they realize in their depths what it means to be Christian, literally to be 'of Christ', and they take responsibility for this opportunity. They are vigilant, they are humble, they are giving, gentle and kind, yet strong and powerful. They are healers and proclaimers of the light. They are joyful transformers of all that is around them. Your devotion to this path puts you here.

Jesus is the one being in whom it is safe to surrender wholeheartedly. No other being can love you as Jesus does. There are no negative effects to loving Jesus, except maybe some disruption due to the changes that can take place in your life, namely, letting go of the negativity that's in your life. Jesus is the great listener, healer, director, and provider. Go to Him with all your needs. His power is forever. His love knows no bounds. Because he is all present and all powerful, he knows everything about you now and everything that will ever be.

To encompass what this beautiful being means to me will take a lifetime to show you. A life of love. This is the intention. And at the same time, I admit, I fall very short in my understanding of Him. I can only know Jesus concordantly with my ability to surrender to love. This love is infinite, powerful, and beyond all imaginings. Suffice to say, I urge you friend: dedicate your heart to Jesus. He will care for it as no one can. This is the best investment you could ever make in your earthly life.

Devotion will bring you close to the heart of Jesus. We are always before the Lord. He is omnipresent. He knows everything about you. He knows your every thought. And yet, He is in love with you. That is a fact. Nothing can change that.

We all feel pain as human beings, and this pain can sometimes direct us to act in ways that aren't considered wholesome. Jesus himself, while on earth, was closest to ones such as these. That is who He seemed to care about most.

It is safe to offer your heart to Jesus. *"Jesus, I'm open. Please show me who you are. Instruct me."*. A simple prayer like this is all that is needed. You will be shown in good time. Remember, you're not just asking anyone, you're asking the One. Keep an open heart and mind, so that you can receive the truth. Remember that God's time is unique. He influences the 10,000 things simultaneously for your benefit. Knowingness and communication will come. Stay patient. Stay inviting.

I'm a songwriter, and if I'm not open to songs coming, they won't. But because of the openness I carry toward the idea of writing songs, over 1,700 songs have come through me. It has been effortless and fun to be a part of the process of creativity in this manner. Only that in the last few years, I don't seem to have the drive to write songs anymore. It is all well and good. There are many ways to touch the Divine.

Opening up and being touched by the Lord is not a logical sequence or happening. It can't be controlled, manipulated or measured. That is because what we can see, our available data, is finite. What the Lord sees is infinite. The greatest beings who have ever touched the earth trusted God resolutely. The fruit of this dedication showered upon us all, as the Love that can only come from God. It is through Love that our thirst is quenched. Historically, this is the only way to be made whole. And for good reason; love is our ultimate Home and Truth. All love comes from the Father.

My heart started burning for the Lord and then I asked Him to be near me. He is always present, it is only I who can stray. So my continuous conversation with Him brings Him into my awareness. It takes me out of my little mind and places me in His loving arms[19].

I love you so much, Lord. Please be with me.
Please guide me. How would you have me, Lord?
I am Thy servant.

---

[19] Psalm 91

Talk like this can go on all day. It gives color to experience. It elevates our thinking and changes our demeanor. I like to use the word "Thy" when addressing the Lord. This is my choice, and I do it out of respect for my Maker.

I stopped in a cathedral to pray recently and afterwards, I went into a coffee shop just down the street. As usual, the place was bustling and there seemed to be only enough space to stand. Suddenly, a vision flashed through my mind. It was of an open seat. I knew exactly where it was. It was the one vacant seat in the whole place. As I walked up the little stairs towards the back entrance, there it was! It's little things like this that reveal how alive life is. There is a greater intelligence at work. Devotion to the Lord is supranormal. It expands our vision of experience and what life is. These things do in fact become part of our life, and after a while become "normal".

Ever notice how when you fall in love with someone you think about them all the time? You want to be with them always. This is what tends to happen to the devoted. We fall in love with the Source of Life. In return, the Lord perfects you into His instrument according to His Will. This happens as we surrender our being to His Being (Good Orderly Direction). The patterns of His Being are not the same patterns that the servant is accustomed to. Our life ultimately becomes both simpler and more profound. So it is.

Without a willingness to change, the path is arduous. However, with the energy of devotion, the willingness is present.

We tend to identify with what we believe life is and who we are. This path will change so many aspects of our experience. It is wise to be ready for anything. It is your front-row seat to the most beautiful journey available.

CHAPTER 4
PRAYER

The Lord is near to all who call on Him,
to all who call on Him in truth.[20]

Prayer is a yearning, an opening up, a communing, and ultimately a portal between the individual self and the Most High. A rocket uses fuel to go beyond the earth's gravity. Prayer is that fuel.

We must not pray by directing God, for that is in error. We must pray by seeking God's will and understanding for us. We seek God's direction in all matters. This is sufficient. If we are faithful in our prayers, if we are willing and devoted, then we will live with ease and assurance. Life becomes simple. Whatever apparent tragedies and struggles that present themselves will undoubtedly be eclipsed with God's helping hands. Have no doubt about this!

---

[20] Psalm 145:18

To the one that abandon's themselves to God in complete trust and faith, peace and beauty are the fruit.

There are two elements involved in moving mountains. The first is faith. Faith in the benevolence and sovereignty of God. The second is prayer. The act of aligning and accepting His Will be done. As we align with the will of God, we find happiness and joy. Our thoughts and prayers become purer, as our personal self recedes. By praying for the highest good of all, we are transformed into an instrument for the highest good for all.

Whether we start the day with the Lord's prayer, with the Prayer of St. Francis, or with a clearing of the mind and communing with God in *holy silence*, the main purpose is that we become empty of self-will, and full of His Will, to the aim of submersion and suffusion with love for God.

If the only intention you carry is to love God, or to love your neighbor… if that be your only objective upon awaking until one goes to sleep… one's life would be a storybook of miracles. An example of God's Power on earth. The people will scarcely believe such a one existed. You will be an inspiration to many.

If you carry conditions on your love for others, that will be your experience of life and God as well. Our experience of self, life, Christ, God, and all other things is connected. There is a single filter through which we see, and everything can only be seen through that filter. This filter is our life energy, which is only changed by spiritual growth. The mind is transformed through our spiritual work because we lose the weight of sin and gain the spirit of heaven through our devotion and love.

The religious often share about their belief system concerning God. However, how we live our life speaks more about what we truly believe. It's impossible for it to be any other way. Professing a perfectly loving God by lip is one thing, knowing a perfectly loving God experientially is another. Which one do you feel has a greater testimony while here on earth? One will not know the God of perfect love until one has been transformed into the likeness of Christ through the state of being called *unconditional love*. Though we are inherently connected and made in the likeness of God, the actual expression of humans varies remarkably. We fall short of the glory of God due to sin. However, we strive to go back to the garden to be with God by the path of love.

I believe sin to be mankind's reliance on himself, reliance on his limited perception, and in the process, his foregoing of his reliance on God. Man felt separate from God and felt he had to make his own way without God. We still make the same mistake every day, and it is this mistake that gives meaning to our life in Christ and that we are trying to correct through our relationship with Him.

Because of original sin, we have needed religion and direction. Their intention is to bring us back to a God that never left us. Doesn't that sound insane? We were created by an Omnipresent God that we are trying to get back to. That's the malady of the "original error"[21]. If Jesus Christ had not taken on human form and

---

[21] the origin of the word sin is "error".

revealed the Reality of God and our relationship to Him through Love, it seems obvious we would have self-destructed a long time ago.

We are a chaotic people fueled by pain and rage, and because of this, we desperately need respite from ourselves. This path, the one of loving without conditions, is the path of rest[22]. It takes a courageous diligence in the beginning, but in due time, just as a rocket leaving earth's gravity, it requires less and less energy to fly onward. It is found that Grace is the guiding force that sustains us on this path. It is also found that all **g**lory is ultimately due to God. I highly recommend having faith in this truth until it presents itself to the servant knowingly.

One major upside of the path of loving without conditions is something called "vision". Vision is the ability to see essence, the inherent truth about a situation or person. It is something akin to intuition. Juxtapose that to the standard judging based off of appearance or past experience.

With growing humility, we see that our perception is limited. When the heart opens and becomes purified through love, less and less do we rely on appearances and the mind's limited data. Through the path of love, we rely more heavily on God by an inner knowingness that is instant, which is a working communication with God. We see that perception is a stumbling block to loving unconditionally. Our reliance on God helps concretize our

---

[22] Matthew 11:28

lovingness into something permanent, unmovable, and longstanding.

The path doesn't end at a certain point, it just gets more profound. It continues onward into new territories of exploration and understanding. God is infinite, therefore our path with God could also be said to be infinite. Reliance on God happens through surrender. We see the truths of the saints and mystics coming true in our own life. St. Paul said, "I live, yet not I… Christ lives within me."[23] We are asking Christ to live through us.

The gift of vision is essentially the discerning of the real from the false. We can see the totality of a situation by bypassing the limitations of the mind. With vision, in a split second, the truth of a situation is revealed. Having the gift of vision still needs to be bridled by our hard-fought spiritual wisdom as temptations and pitfalls surely await.

There are social movements in the world that would like to take the word "God" out of every aspect of our public lives. There would no doubt be major consequences to the world for such a thing to happen. Perhaps there are those who have been affected negatively by organized religion in the name of God. This is obviously due to the errors of humans and has nothing to do with God Himself.

God is beyond description, beyond male and female, and beyond mental comprehension. What we can say about God is that

---

[23] Galatians 2:20

to align with Him is to live in harmony within oneself and with nature. The startling revelation of God in one's own life is profoundly transformative. Afterwards, one is never the same again.

I remember the necessity of having to take a religion credit in college to meet a graduation requirement. It was my sophomore year and I was not 100% excited to do this. While I was glancing at a syllabus on my way across campus, a woman I had never had a conversation with came out of nowhere. She exclaimed, "You should take *Studies in Religion* with Ms. Solberg."

How did she know I was looking for a religion credit at that moment? There was no way for her to see what I was looking at, as she was coming from the other direction. Regardless, I listened.

It turned out that the class grabbed my attention from the get go. I admired the brilliant minds of the students in discussions. "Wow, people actually think about this stuff," I remember thinking. Through my young adulthood, I had not given serious thought to the topic. I was about to go through monumental change and didn't know it.

The professor asked us: *"What is truth?"* and *"How do you know what you've been spoon-fed is the truth?"* That was all I needed to hear. My jaw dropped to the floor and I was speechless in the class for about the next month or two. A transformation was happening that I couldn't begin to understand, but something inside of me liked it.

There I was, driving along highway 169 outside St. Peter, Minnesota. I turned off the music and was suddenly experiencing an inner dilemma. I started praying out loud: "God, I'm told believe in this, or I will go to hell. A person in China is told by their parents to believe differently, and that that is their truth. What makes my belief system better or even right? How can I even know truth? This all seems like a big [expletive] joke!", I yelled out.

At that moment, I experienced something powerful. A bright, shining light shone in front of my car. A fleeting thought arose: "Was I seeing a shooting star?" It was clear it was something out of the ordinary, and it startled me. Then a wave of peace came over my being. Tears started pouring down my cheeks. Out of my mouth came the words, "God, I don't know what you are... but I will stay open."

Divinity had answered my call in that moment, and it struck me powerfully to my core. This firmly catapulted me into the "belief in God" camp. Little did I know that that day would be a pinnacle moment that helped start a long journey for me in knowing God. It could be no other way.

I spent the next few months dissecting my beliefs. What did I really believe? I intuited that I needed to let go of everything that I was taught about life and God. I needed to start from a clean slate. In the process of laying down the things I had adhered to and accepted, I found that there was one at the bottom that I couldn't let go of... and I had tried. I didn't know why, it was just there. I had a love for Christ that I could not separate from my very being.

Pray Without Ceasing

The bible advises us to "pray without ceasing".[24] How can this be done? We live busy lives, would this not interfere with our ability to function properly in this complex world?

My understanding is that we are always praying, no matter what we are doing, no matter where we are. We are always before God. It is written that "not a sparrow falls without His knowing", and "every hair on your head is counted". This tells us that God is in fact omniscient, by nature of His being God. He does not only hear us when we fold our hands.

When we align with the path of loving without conditions, we come to realize that we have times in our life when we are surely less than loving. There are pockets where we are acting out of erroneous beliefs, inner pain or repressed traumas. These often come out of us as judgements and anger. We want to heal these areas. To do so means to make them conscious so we might go beyond them. That may sound daunting, but what we are really doing in the process is taking away the things that take us away from God, for instance: judgements, resentments, shame, guilt, hatred, anger and pride.

It is patience and steadfastness that takes one to the goal. The adage "one day at a time" applies here. As soon as we wake up in the morning, we are aware that we are before God, so our mind turns to Him immediately. With everyone that we encounter, to our times alone, we are with God. God is the best friend we can ever have. God is unconditional love and much more. We reap

---

[24] 1 Thessalonians 5:16-18

the results of our own choices, but God does not gloat in our suffering. God is unlimited hope and inspiration. We go through our peaks and valleys, but God does not change. We keep the compass set on God's love, day in and day out. God will always be there. It is we who change, not God. It is within the changeful that we can come to realize the presence of God, which is found to be love itself, always present with us.

In a later chapter various prayers are shared for directing our spirit towards God. But in this chapter, it's enough to speak about what prayer means. We can use formal prayer as a lever to shift our orientation in the moment towards heaven. However, times without formal prayer are not less important. Prayer is the act of love. St. Therese of Lisieux said it best: "Without love, deeds, even the most brilliant, count as nothing." This is where we aim, to be always before God, to be in communication with Him, and to see Him always. The state of love is literally seeing *with* God.

What ultimately comes of the path of loving without conditions? You will know a joy beyond this world from your relationship with God. From this joy comes tremendous energy and insight. Joy is a beacon unto man saying, "this is the way." In truth, many are repelled by it because they are so out of touch with their innocent nature. However, our path still blesses all life, seen and unseen. Our time here is fleeting, let us be about our Father's business!

CHAPTER 5
BEAUTY

Blessed are the pure in heart,
for they shall see God.[25]

There is always beauty before us. For many, it comes at a peak life moment, for the better or worse, to reveal the perfection and beauty of the moment.

We've all heard the saying that "time stood still" when someone fell in love. Another saying is "you don't know what you've got until it's gone." At times of tremendous loss, the beauty of the thing we've lost immediately comes to mind. Most that have been to a funeral understand this.

Unfortunately, in mundane life, we often need to 'wake up' to see the beauty that is always right before us. Remember falling in love with someone? The clarity we felt, the intensity of colors, the

---

[25] Matthew 5:8

beauty of the person, the majesty all around, there was a perfection to the moment. We truly felt "alive". Perception was quieted and the beauty of the moment bled through.

In moments of being touched by beauty, what has actually altered is merely our outlook. There is a suspension of judgement. The loving are this way, they allow things to be as they are. They lift a situation just by being present to it. Others know when they are being loved because they feel free.

The path of Loving Without Conditions is synonymous with the path of beauty. How can that be? Because in learning to love, we are learning to let go of our reliance on limiting perception. The mind says: "oh, I know that tree." All the past associations with trees are involved in seeing a single tree. If one is not seeing beauty, one is actually not looking at a tree at all; one is looking at the past.

Seeing through the eyes of our spirit, which is functionally what happens in the state of love, we look at the same exact tree we passed over previously, but this time, we see its perfection. I mean, imagine that! There are these gorgeous structures all around us, reaching up into the heavens. Revealing their splendor in the spring with the birth of new life. Revealing plushness and fruits in the summer. Revealing luminous colors and decay in the fall. Revealing naked stability in the winter. Just sitting there, ever so steady. Works of art. All art is trying to imitate what nature does effortlessly. Have you noticed the beauty of a tree lately? People are no different. The beauty of people is everywhere. All people. This fact is only hidden by the judging mind.

If you did nothing else but held the intention to see the beauty of life, you would fulfill Christ's teaching. Beauty is love. To see the inner innocence of life is to see its beauty. Jesus could look through the appearance and see to essence. This is what love reveals. Our essence is spirit and innocence. You cannot see someone's beauty and not love them profoundly.

A parent loves their child even after the child has done something harmful or malicious. The parent may be disappointed, but the parent loves the child regardless. Even later, when the child is an adult, the parent can see the little child within them, the innocence that the adult will always be.

When we are willing to sacrifice our programming and judgment, we can open our hearts to what is present. This is the wager of love. We let go of our selfishness, and we get to see through the eyes of heaven. To see from the mind is to see through a pre-programmed lens, which is to see something dead and no longer existent. A loving mind can use the wisdom of the past while seeing the clarity of the present.

As we examine and let go of our own self judgements, we start to see our own beauty, lovability, and innocence. There is beauty innate to our existence. Sometimes we need to heal from previously held trauma, but we can give ourselves our support for this impressive job it takes to be a human. Every person is like a work of art, even what the world calls "ugly." It is not in some people more than others. However, it does shine through each of us to varying degrees. The journey to love is the hard-fought give for humanity. Let your light so shine!

We see the beauty and innocence of others, but we never lose site of the capability of an individual to do evil. To be loving does not mean to be naive. We can see this evil in others because we are in touch with the capability of evil inside ourselves. We are aware of it, but we don't fear it. We respect it, but we don't run from it. With love, we forgive the innate, animalistic drives that exist within us. When they do express, we smile at them. They can't help but be what they are. Someone pulled out in front of you in traffic? The knee jerk reaction was, "you fool!". And yet, we see that we are not that action. We take responsibility for this part of us. We ask the Lord for help in forgiving and accepting this part of us. Love truly does heal all.

Beauty holds an element of "awe" within it, but it also holds a high level of gratitude. When we see beauty, we are already feeling grateful. Are you aware of the ground under your feet? Are you aware there is an atmosphere for you to breathe in? Are you aware of all the processes that are going on inside your body, helping to make it function? It's amazing to think that when you are thirsty you can simply go get water from the tap. How is this even possible? You didn't do any of it. Are you aware that you didn't create your own existence? You exist because of something greater than you. There is beauty in all this.

When I was younger, I took all this for granted. It seems that the older I get, I'm hard-pressed to find a day go by that I'm not feeling blessed, to the point of awe, for my existence and all the ingredients that make up this life. We are blessed beyond our recognition.

True gratitude arises in the moment. There may be inspiration swelling in the heart. It may take the form of a song, a jig, a glance, a bright word, an attitude, even a cry… you might find your heart glowing. When we begin to see how much we rely on God for everything, how can we not be grateful?

Spirituality, at its core, is a process of stripping away the unnecessary. In the beginning, we might read a lot of books and take in a lot of information. As we become more seasoned and satiate the thirst of the mind, we find that to attain the heights of spiritual connection to God, we actually need to die to what we think we know.[26]

We may have learned so much through the years only to realize how simple life actually is. How beautiful life is and always will be. How precious we are in the sight of God, and how sacred our life is. The awareness of love is not something we create, but more something that is revealed. God is love. We are enveloped by His grace.

Some of the most profound stages of our spiritual calling are the dropping away of unnecessary baggage. For many of us, it can feel like these are periods of trial. Jesus calls us to put down the false parts of ourselves.[27] On the other side of such "purgations"

---

[26] Matthew 18:3
[27] John 15:13

comes clarity, and awareness of beauty arises. These times reaffirm the reason we are on this path.

In my own path, there came the awareness that I no longer resisted the "trying" times, and I no longer sought after the "good" times. They are actually the same. Perception will say they are different, but that's just due to our emotions. In truth, God is. Everything else changes and is therefore not of God. That which is of God is forever the same. A world without end, amen.

We tend to resist the "dying" phases. We want to hold onto what we know and who we think we are. This attitude obviously holds back our spiritual growth. Hopefully, we have a pact with Jesus that is stronger, to which we say "yes" to the resistant times aided through our devotion. We choose to endure temporary discomfort for the greater rewards. We trust Him more than we trust our false sense of security. Jesus continually takes our hand and leads us into where we haven't been, ultimately new dimensions of love and freedom. We are much bigger than we could ever imagine. Likewise, life is so much bigger than we could imagine. Beauty is all around, and what a joy and opportunity to be able to be open to this. In doing so, we are serving God and man because that's where the suffering person wants to be. In beauty, around beauty, and forever... beauty.

The choice for forgiveness and the act to surrender our will can be hard-fought at times. Bullet-proof trust and faith in our Higher Power will eventually see us through. It is this process where life changes most rapidly, and we discover the sweeter fruits. One eventually finds that all fear and limitation is an appearance and that it's safe to surrender and walk through the fear. On the other side of fear is found the beauty that the fear masked. We have been free all along.

The seeing of beauty tells you: *all is well*.

One of my earliest memories of being moved by the beauty of music was when I was around 5 years old. I went into my father's truck and put in one of his tapes. On came Louis Armstrong's "What a Wonderful World". There was a timelessness that encompassed me and tears flowed down my cheeks. This again happened many times in my youth. Music has always been a powerful tool that has lifted my being up into the realms of beauty and love.

In my home, I tend to play enchanting music while I drink coffee or pray. Music that is loving can be inspiring and help set a devotional environment. This often happens at live concerts as well, where the spirit of the music is often conveyed most powerfully.

My dad would often invite me to listen to music with him while I was growing up. This was a way we connected with beauty together. He was not afraid to let himself feel the essence of the song deeply and would often weep. He resonated with the words of music most often. He would tell me, "listen to the words. I went to write over a thousand songs in my life. The openness to receiving the songs, which is how it literally feels, was the opportunity to be a part of and to share in beauty.

Exercise: Before you leave the house today, notice your beauty. Even the beauty of aging. When you meet people outside the house notice their beauty.   In the process, you'll see a suspension of judgment and an openness in your heart. The sounds all around you are heightened and pleasant, and nature is more alive than ever.   This is the gift of loving without conditions because it's the gift of knowing God's Presence.

CHAPTER 6
HEALING

I will come and heal him.[28]

Jesus is the greatest healer and displayer of true power this world has ever known. His miracles were used to awake a sleeping people to the truth of God. What is more, the miracles happened. What was written of Him in the Bible happened. He fed the multitude. He healed the lame. He walked on water. We can only come to this truth by grace. The knowing of these things as true takes place in our own being because of our walk with Him. We intuit God's power, and/or experience similar miracles for ourselves. How do these things happen in our life? -*We get out of the way and we invite God in.* Which is itself, the core of all spirituality. God's love is powerful and always there, shining in,

---

[28] Matthew 8:7

around, and through us... We come to find these things happen now and always.

Countless others since that time have performed miracles of healing in Jesus' name. They believed in Him so fully, and allowed His Spirit to heal through them for others. The writer of this book has done the same. Because of his faith in Jesus, he has taken part in many healings, even bringing the once dead back to life. All in Jesus' name and by His Word. Not only because of faith, but due to trust and abidance in Him. The acceptance of what *God is*— is what is in awareness for these things to happen. That knowingness is wordless. It just is. We become aware of this relationship due to our alignment with spiritual truth. It is what this book is about. That we may align with the Spirit of Truth, God Almighty!

In this chapter, I wanted to speak about love in regards to healing. I will put it succinctly in two ways: *Love is the ultimate law of life*, and L*ove heals all*. Love and God cannot be separated. It is when we submit to darkness, as in the happenings of suicide and depression, that we are most cut off from God knowingly. It is true that love defies measurement, reason, and any parameters we could set upon it. There are observable qualities of the expression of love, but they are not always predictable.

Love is abundant, even infinite. It is the real power of this universe. Everything else can run dry, but love will always remain. Things may seem dark, but that is only so because our perception says so. Love will always prevail for the faithful. Those with faith will always prove this truth.

You are not separate from the Source of Love. That is why we can heal in Jesus' name. If I come and go with Jesus alone, I come with infinite possibility and power. And I do nothing! He does the works. I am just faithful. I have said "yes" to God. The rest is Him.

There is nothing more powerful and affirming than a heart full of divine love. It changes the whole world just because it has been realized by one person. Miracles are normal. Their happening reminds us of His Infinite Splendor. They are not necessary, but they are the automatic consequence of truth replacing falsity. They revive the heart, uplift the fallen, and help bring those gone astray back home. They are a reminder of His timeless Love. They are a response to the answer. The answer is this: God is love.

You are inherently a miracle worker! Does that mean you should head out of your house with a cape today? Of course not. The mere understanding that God is, and God being Omnipotent, is surely enough. It brings calm to the heart. If God wills that a miracle happen with your involvement, it will come to pass. That being said, it tends to come to pass through the faithful, the loyal, the devotional and those surrendered to His Will. But again, God is not predictable, and because we don't have the amount of information God has, our perspective is limited. If you allow God to live your life, you will soar. This is what this path is, a surrender and a faith. How I live my life is my prayer. *God's will be done... not mine.*

To the unfaithful, it sounds like misery to submit to something other than oneself. To the loyal, it is heaven. The more devoted and seasoned we are on the path of love, the more we become aware of the continuity of the Presence of God. What the world calls "miracles" becomes commonplace. We can then be said to live in this world, but we are not of this world. In this world we are chosen by God, being His own. However, we also need to accept the calling. We choose for love, God, truth, forgiveness, surrender, clarity, compassion, true knowing... We do not choose its corollary, which is hell.

With the highs of love can come the low's of being away from our Beloved, ie., not feeling spiritual blessings or not feeling "in the flow" with life. However, these times are opportunities. That which is not of love comes up in our awareness. This can often take time to see through.

We tend to resist that which brings suffering. However, this prolongs our suffering. Instead, we can choose to welcome and accept whatever the Lord of Love brings us. As pain and resistance are swallowed up by our acceptance of them, also aided by our devotion to God, we realize how temporary all experience is. In due time, we see that there is no reason to cling to any idea or experience, for they are limited and temporary. The ebbs and flows of life, and the pain and the joys, are fleeting. They both tend to become accepted for what they are. We realize we can't control the flow of life, we can only choose to flow with it.

When we become surrendered to God's will, we realize everything is doing its best. In fact, everything is perfect. It's all part of a larger symphony. It is in resisting 'what is' that leads to suffering. To accept this truth and to flow with life is to live a life in peace and abidance in God's Holy Will. We are blessed to even see this as a possible way to live. There is no better life possible than when one strives to serve God. God is the Hand that writes the pen. And this story already has a final ending. We need to play our part. The most romantic parts are the ones where people give their whole hearts to God. You are part of a love story right now. May God bless your every breath.

All life is an appearance. God, the essence of life, doesn't change. That is why our North Star is God. It is unwise of us to set our hopes on objects of this world that will fade away. Just as much as we do, it will be our folly. To come to know the source of your existence is sheer joy and peace. That is God. And that should be sought above all else. Your realization of this principal is the ultimate gift to the world because it is beyond suffering. To be with God is to be in heaven. Heaven is the only place free from suffering.

The experience of the human being is physical, mental, and spiritual. We are responsible to care for this body. We do so. Let us be careful not to give the body too much importance, for they are temporary objects. Extremes are often forms of mental and spiritual disease. Too much exercise, eating too little, fear of germs, etc., are some examples. Too much preoccupation with the body will not bless your body. Life actually works very well when we stay out of its way. It is often we who disrupt the natural rhythms of life. Be responsible, but not anxious. Love the body, but don't obsess about it. The body will take care of itself with adequate food, adequate rest, and adequate maintenance.

We will all shed our mortal physicality. People that exercise incessantly often do not live longer than people who are much more moderate with health preoccupation. Look to the Lord in everything, that is where answers await. When you are healthy in mind and spirit, the physical will follow suit. By being balanced and healthy in life, we intuitively know how to deal with situations.

One spiritual trap is complete neglect of the body. It's easy to do this when we start to feel the peace of the Lord and we begin to see that we are actually not our bodies. That our existence as spirit is much more real and eternal. This brings with it much joy. And still, this is our vessel to spread the beautiful fragrance of Jesus in this world. A tool to heal the lame. People suffer greatly here. Let us love it all with a holy love, as the Lord wills for us. There is no greater path of meaning that exists for us on this planet. Those that take it will have the greatest party when it is time to shed the body. What we love, we become.

Can we be honest with ourselves about what we fear? The huge advantage when getting honest with our fears is that then they can be healed and forgiven. It is this very thing that may be causing some problems in one's life. It can seem counter-productive to actively look at our fears at first. Our natural instinct is often to push away what doesn't feel pleasant. It is this pushing away that gives power to fear. It is our fears and resistances that often will affect our health in ways initially unseen. What we choose not to look at about ourselves is where our physical dilemmas often arise. On the path of loving without conditions, these mental and spiritual obstacles naturally present themselves to us.

In loving without conditions, we love all life. To let a fear be what it is, essentially to accept it, allows the fear to do the thing we would like it to do: vanish. All fear vanishes when we accept the fear, no matter how it appears and how it makes us feel. We tackle it head-on. We bow to it and say "yes". This doesn't mean the fear will happen, it more so means "I won't be dominated by you in my psyche any longer."

We act from a place of acceptance. We have more freedom from accepting the situation as we find it. We allow the fear to be what it is without trying to change it. As an aid to surrender, I see myself as a soldier on a battlefield. For a higher purpose, I surrender my life. Like at the beginning of the movie "Dances With Wolves", where Kevin Costner rides a horse between the North and the South. He literally surrenders his life. This is the choice every day. Accept the choice to be a servant of God. May our devotion and love for God keep us close to Him!

Intense prayer, coupled with surrender to God's will, is often the precursor to the miraculous. When you realize that God is all that is, and that it is the Father's pleasure to "give you the Kingdom", the conscious awareness of God itself can heal.

One time my father had an extremely swollen and also dislocated ankle. He couldn't walk at all and could put zero pressure on it. This had happened before and he claimed he couldn't walk for a few weeks. He jokingly asked me to "pop it back in place". At the time, as a young man, I had been newly "on fire" for the Lord and dwelling on the works of Jesus in the Bible. Jesus' words were piercing my heart. In response to him, I said: "I'm no doctor, dad. But I know it can be healed if you believe." He received me and said, "alright."

I went straight down to my room to pray and fell to my knees. With a deep surrender and longing towards the Lord, in this moment, I recognized that the power which created the entire universe was still just as present with me right now and always would be. If God was present with me (Omnipresent), then He was also present with my dad as well. What appears as an "ankle", a thing separate from God, is just my idea. *God is.* In that moment, all went silent...even breathing stopped momentarily. Then I found myself taking a long, deep breath. I said, "Thank you Lord". Then I surrendered the whole situation to the Lord and went to bed.

The next morning my dad came out of his room beaming from head to toe, with his body in perfect working order. He even hopped on the healed foot. This experience affirmed my already intuited belief. I saw that the realization of God on this earth was the greatest gift I could give to others.

Miracles happen when truth replaces falsity. That is why those of us on the path of refining our love are potential miracle workers. As we adhere to the Lord, we bring that vision down to the earth. We bring order to chaos. We bring silence to noise. We bring calm to the storm. To love without conditions is a blessing to all people, whether they know it or not. God will not be seen through the eyes of judgement. God is perceived through the eyes of love.

The Lord said: *These things and more ye shall do.*[29] This is a true statement. But what I find interesting is that when these things have happened in my life, it's like they were just known to be true before they even happened. Because of this, I surmise the statement "God's will be done" in those situations. It was like a feeling in the moment, "yes, this is to be," a knowingness. This *knowing* comes with deep surrender and abidance with God.

I met a young woman once when I was playing acoustic music outdoors at a bar in Rochester, Minnesota. We felt a connection immediately. I remember we seemed to both feel awe-struck and speechless. No words were exchanged, but she handed me her telephone number. A few days later, she invited me to her apartment for tea. Upon entering, I was intuitively aware of something "higher" going on. I couldn't put my finger on it, but I could feel it. I remember feeling like there were angels present as I walked into her flat.

---

[29] John 14:12

She seemed agitated. So I asked her, "What's wrong?" She said her pet fish had died earlier that day, as it floated upside down in her fishbowl. For whatever reason, she said that it had come to her during a trying time and was important to her. Out from my mouth, without even thinking, came the words: "I don't think it has to die". Intuitively, I held both my hands a short distance on each side of the small aquarium it was floating in. After maybe 10 seconds, the upside down, dead fish started blinking its eyes. And after about 30 seconds, I removed my hands. In around a minute or two it was again swimming around freely in its bowl. It was now completely alive and healthy.

In moments such as these, time sort of stills. The perfection and beauty of the moment are all that is real. It appears we came together just for this experience. Afterwards, we only saw each other one or two more times. She gifted me a diary at Plum's Bar in St. Paul, at a music concert of mine. Inside the diary is inscribed, "thank you for saving my fish."

We may not always know the "why" of events, but I surmise the fish was healed in front of her because it was God's will for us to be a part of this event. I'm content letting it be what it is and giving to God all the glory. Thankfully, even at that young age, I was open to the miraculous and aware that I could not claim ownership. Glory was given to God and the mind did not take credit, which is one spiritual temptation we must be careful not to fall into when we are a part of the miraculous. The miraculous can happen at any time in our life, but we must bring the presence of God with us, which opens us to that which is beyond this world. We always give all glory to God.

All the power to move mountains is present with us. But knowledge of that power is worthless if it isn't aligned with God's Will. **How to know God's Will?** That's easy; ask for it and open oneself to God inwardly with *knowingness*. The knowingness says, "I love God. I trust God. Thou art." Know what I mean? We can live in this way. Being with God in all the departments of our life. It's the great love affair we never knew we were longing for.

Like a tuning fork, when we commit to this relationship with God, He aligns us the way He sees fit. Life becomes simpler. He helps us be in harmony with Him. He is the peace, love, and joy for us that we always yearned for. We trust in God and that He will provide what we are insufficient of ourselves.

We must not be attached to outcomes, to preconceived ideas of how things "should go". We can only see a small number of criteria in any given situation. But there is literally a plethora of information that would be needed to make an accurate assessment of a single event or thing. In truth, there are no events. The Presence of God is beyond all time, and thank God for this, because then He is always available and present. God is the Great Context, knowing everything for all time, by sheer fact of being Creator. He is always present as benevolence, but also as justice. Since God is context, and nothing escapes His view, we bow to His Will. We don't have to be the judge, jury, and executioner of this world (thankfully).

We watch ourselves, and when we think we are big, we pray to be brought back to balance. In seeing rightly, in our smallness, we can be bold. To be with God is to be fearless. It is through our reliance on God that greatness comes.

When we fail, we give glory to God. We needn't understand all outcomes. We simply do our best. *"Thy will be done Lord, not mine"*. We accept 'what is'. This orientation to life, of giving God the glory, keeps us humble and supplies us with what we need to do His bidding. The moment we surrender our personal will to Him is the moment of the true miracle. Miracles are continuous and always present. The mere fact that you experience existence is the first miracle of life. From Nothingness, came Something. Be humble. Be grateful. Be willing. Be open. God will do the rest.

When we drive around in our car, we know that God is in charge. When we are in the grocery line, we know that God is in charge. Whomever we encounter, God is in charge. We believe that the moment is pregnant with the abundance of joy, the spontaneous, and a deep love beyond what we can understand. That is the moment. That is to be alive. We have a front-row seat to the extraordinary, and it was right where we always were. It can never not be. Do you understand this is where your deep meaning and purpose lie yet? Do not go to sleep. Wake up! There is so much work to be done. Let us begin.

CHAPTER 7
FORGIVENESS

Blessed are the merciful,
for they shall receive mercy.[30]

Forgiveness is key to inner peace and wellbeing. Without it, we cannot fulfill the teaching of Christ. In my experience, it is not understood en masse. The mechanics of it are often unknown. The idea of forgiveness, which is essentially to let go of, to let pass, or to overlook, is what the follower of Christ must understand and accomplish. Sounds great, right? It is great! However, when holding a cherished judgement or grievance in real time, forgiveness can be a struggle. It's a hard thing to begin to do for the average person that is accustomed to clinging on to what they see as "reality". But it can be done, and it can become a way of living; to forgive. When anything less than love arises in our

---

[30] Matthew 5:7

experience, a little awareness within us raises a flag and says, "Hey, you might want to look at this... is this really aligned with love?" The willingness to do so comes from the heart and is fueled by devotion to God, love, and our fellow beings.

I would like to offer a new definition of forgiveness, which is: *to see the innocence of.* What I mean by this is to abide in a devotional *state of being* known as *unconditional love* by intending to see the innocence of all life. There are no mental exercises necessary to be in this place. You don't need to see a "bad" person make a "bad" action and then say, "Well, I forgive you even though it was bad." To see the innocence of life is to see that all life is doing its best. A thing can't help but be what it is. And if it could do better, it would. Since life is doing its best, even when it appears awful, that's forgivable. And if I see the innocence of life, what is there to forgive? Living in unconditional love is living in a space where forgiveness has already taken place outside of time. It becomes a way of being in Christ.

There is a great amount of energy we will save when we have tackled the things that we repress and don't want to deal with. Much of the time we are re-hashing the past and trying to work things out in our mind. This comes into play in our adult life when we repeat childhood patterns in relationships.

When we forgive, energy is freed up. The ability to focus on the moment at hand is more fluid and automatic. There is more energy to simply "be". That is where the joys of life are found, and that is why this is a path of joy.

The kind of forgiveness I am speaking of is one where forgiveness has already taken place before any action is even committed. We dwell in a wondrous power called "love". It is always present. To do this, as mentioned in a previous chapter, we must not see through the body's eyes only, but with surrender to God and a reliance on the Holy Spirit for seeing. This is done through our devotion and communion with God and the Holy Spirit.

If you hadn't realized it already, forgiveness is literally "laying down your life for your friends."[31]   Forgiveness is setting something aside that we normally won't: ourselves. It takes great courage to do so, in fact, it takes God's grace to even begin to do so in the first place.

We have relied on our perception all our life, and we think we need it to survive. As we evolve in our spiritual relationship with God, our perception changes and begins to look different. *Essence* begins to present itself more readily: what is true in a situation, as opposed to faulty perception based off of appearances.

When you feel a judgement, or should a shortsighted thought arise, lean on the Lord: "Father, I do not see clearly. Please help me see this situation as you would have me." If we are willing to let go of our limited view and welcome a new view with abandonment to the Holy Spirit, a new outlook will come. It is normally accompanied by a courageous feeling of wellbeing and clarity.

We cannot see the perfection in a situation while we bring our past into the present. In other words, we tend to see through a distorted lens. A program (based on the past) is not real in the

---

[31] John 15:13

moment. Though we learn from our experience of the past, it is also limited and distorted to think that would necessarily give an accurate assessment of the present. And isn't what we saw in the past also based off of our programming then?

To be truly creative and alive, we must be open to the moment, not carrying the load of the past expressed as judgements and limiting positions. This is often why artists have a love-hate relationship with their art. They'll go through a slump in productivity only to release into the high of a productive time. This high is a release from the constrictions imposed by oneself (the past), and an openness to what is new at this moment. The moment is always fresh, always alive, and always abundant. To abide in this abundance is to be present to this moment, where true vision resides.

One of the reasons there is so much complexity in the world nowadays, is because we are an overly mind heavy people. We spend less time actually being in our bodies and with each other, and more time is spent in our minds. The mind can go down a million rabbit holes. It can miss the forest for the trees, so to speak. We get lost in our limiting, conceptual mazes.

Most minds are predictable. The gift of vision that comes from the path of loving without conditions cuts through the morass and reveals *essence*. It is effortless, it is easy, and it is fun. Judging the world via our programming feels safe. You can't have an open heart in this world and be judging at the same time. With vision, you learn to work with your intuition. You know when something feels right, it just "clicks". The Holy Spirit is itself infinite knowledge. To rely on the Holy Spirit for vision is found to be true security. We are not alone.

What I love about interacting with children is their innocence and the opportunity to bathe in it with them. What I love about adolescence is the awakening of their intellect, their excitement in the discovery of life and its symbols. They carry a wonder that is freeing. What I love about the late teens and college years is that I often find an openness to them. With it, a spontaneous joy to connect with and a glow that's available to share. What I love about the latter 20s and 30s is that I feel a shared life experience. There's an understanding: "life is hard, but we are figuring it out." With those in their 40s and 50s, we can find a deepening wisdom of life and a deepening acceptance of how life works. It's fun to share in the subtleties of their perception. I often find with those in their 60s and beyond a deeper letting go and less of a need to control things, people, and situations. Aspects of our youth, especially in the 70s and 80s, often start to return: a glow and a mesmerizing joy. The most beautiful people, to me, are our elders. How could they not be? Imagine all they've seen and lived through. All the experiences they have to share. And when you see their beauty, you see the beauty of all the ages.

At every stage in life, we can totally connect with joy, innocence, and beauty. Everyone carries it, but often people are cut off from it. This is usually due to what's rummaging through their mind in what they have left to tackle and heal in their life (perhaps shame, anger, or grief). Thankfully, joy is contagious and free. A wide-open gaze and a smile can melt through almost any exterior wall we carry.

When the practice of forgiveness becomes a consistent part of your life, life readily shines with holiness and beauty. A space is created. You feel lighter. Your inner life becomes at least as important as the outer world of appearances. You can get accustomed to that joyful space, and when you are not in it, there is a yearning to get back there. So we look forward to the opportunities to grow. We do this for love of God and this world of suffering people. The purgation of our smallness surely brings good.

Since God is the Creator, and literally the Light of Life, when we judge the world, we are dissecting God's creation and even judging God. But don't worry, God can take it! (Insert smiley face emoji) We are on a path to learn to love *all life*, not just what is convenient. Regardless of deeds, everything is innately innocent simply because the essence of that life is God. And where there is evil, "Father forgive them. They know not what they do."[32]

We are life. When we abuse and sin, we abuse and sin against all life. That same life, beyond the differences in appearance, is in

---

[32] Luke 23:24

everyone. There is nothing created that is not "of God".[33] We are not separate from or disenfranchised from God. If such a thing could ever be said to exist, it is only in the mind of conceptual thought.

Ultimately, what is done against Him is done against ourselves.[34] What is done against ourselves is done against Him. You didn't create your own life, you don't have the power of creation. None of us do. However, we do have the power of Creation within us.[35] When we live aligned with God's laws, we live aligned with Him, and that is Power. Forgiveness is the means that we align with God. To judge life is to live unaligned with God and Power.

We use our free will to know and choose for God. Others will use their free will to go against God. Pride, vanity, cruelty and corruption have their own rewards. We are to avoid these things at all costs, that we may forgive this world and be free. Our forgiveness is our gift of love to the world. What an amazing legacy we have at our hands.

How to forgive? Simple: "Heavenly Father, please help me to see this [person, place, thing, etc.] differently." If one is willing to let go of their current and limited way of seeing, being, or doing, and open up to God for assistance, then the Holy Spirit will

---

[33] John 1:3
[34] Psalm 82:6; John 10:34
[35] Luke 17:21

transform one's heart and mind into something much more calm and expansive, much more meaningful and beautiful. You can be the change you so desperately want to see in the world. When we are willing to let go of our need to be right and welcome the Holy Spirit, the Holy Spirit takes care of the rest.

You may notice that some pain sticks with us for longer periods. It is a difficult task to forgive some deep and embedded circumstances. For instance, you may have forgiven a parent, and yet there is still a feeling of unease surrounding your experience with them. Some experiences have been stored away since early childhood. We call this trauma. To access the trauma, in order to heal and go beyond, we need outside help. This topic will be addressed again towards the later part of this book with potential resources.

When I was a boy, it was obvious that my dad held his father with some disgust. It appeared my grandfather had done horrendous things, which was likely coupled with an undiagnosed alcoholism. It seemed to me that my father had pushed down the pain, not knowing how to deal with it. Occasionally, when we worked together around the house, I remember him speaking from this pain. He did not hold back his words of anger, sometimes with spit flying from his mouth. The little boy I was would watch this with amazement.

Somehow along the way, I too felt resistance and anger towards my own father. When I went away to college, I went through changes. I was no longer looking at my dad the same, and I told him. Standing outside his bedroom one evening before bed, I boldly said, "Dad, I don't know why, but I have hatred in my heart for you. I know you had it for your father as well. But I will not run from it. I'm going to get to the bottom of this." I wanted to heal this pattern that I saw and felt.

By this time, I was well along on my spiritual path and devoted to love, growth, and healing. However, it took me about 13 more years to resolve that pain within myself! I had to unlock these stored away feelings. Once this was done, I could begin to heal and let go of it.

When visiting my dad in my early 30s, I was excited to share with him about my life. I opened my heart to him and when I finished, he just looked the other way like I had just said nothing. The normal feeling for me would be to feel let down and angry. Suddenly, from the depths of my being forgiveness arose and the words came out; "I love you dad."

That was a turning point. There was complete acceptance of him and the situation. My dad was mentally forgiven at this point. However, I still had emotional baggage that I didn't understand. Upon joining a 12-step group, working the 12 steps of recovery, and speaking openly with others about these issues, the healing came. While driving along one day, I was listening to some 12-step testimonials. The man speaking, an alcoholic, told the audience that when his son joined AA himself, they all became the first father his son ever had. Suddenly, out of the depths of my being, I cried out: "I never had a father."

My mind previously would not allow such a thought to arise because my dad was always there. What I grieved was his emotional absence. He was emotionally absent for me. This was likely due to the fact that his own father was emotionally absent for him, and he had not yet resolved this pain within himself. He was doing his best, but I felt the loss and resultant pain. At that moment, I allowed myself to experience the emotion that accompanied this realization to its end. Essentially, there was a long and deep cry.

Afterwards, I was left with nothing but peace and gratitude for my father. He was beautiful all along. I could see him clearly now. The lens of hurt was gone. I saw him for what he was: a beautiful man doing the best he could under the conditions of his life. From then onward, there has been loving him for who he is, not who I thought he should be. Now I feel blessed by the relationship. I feel lucky to continue our journey of love together.

When we first open up to the field of love, it's truly incredible. I remember being aware of love, but also that there were conditions on my love. Since my goal was loving without conditions, this was painful. I sincerely wanted to make that love pure, as a gift to my Lord. It ached my heart so much to see limitations arise. I would pray and ask God to show me any conditions on my love for life. Inevitably, something would arise.

I once prayed, "Lord, do I have limitations on my love?" At that moment, there was nothing that I could recall. By the time I finished that prayer, the lady I was renting from came powerfully to mind. She was somehow disgruntled toward me. It was so painful. Somehow this was reflecting something inside me, a limitation on my love. I prayed about this rigorously and prayed for her. Eventually, she revealed that I reminded her of the one man in her life that had broken her heart. It seemed I would trigger her. The limits on my love with her were found to be that I was taking offense when she was not reciprocating my goodwill towards her. I was essentially feeling like a victim.

What's unique and fascinating about this path is that the patterns of our life are changed significantly. Things line up to aid us on our way. Sometime down the road, after I had moved on from that home with the landlord, she was placed perfectly in my path in a grocery store parking lot. I hugged her, told her she looked beautiful and wished her well. But I did not want anything from her, emotionally, in return. The meeting was a symbol of healing for me.

My limitations on love have often had to do with unconscious guilt and shame. There were things I needed to forgive but didn't yet have access to. I think in my early spiritual journey I wanted to cling onto the highs of the Lord, and not go into my "shadow" work. I was hoping these things would heal or vanish on their own. Ultimately, I knew I needed some form of therapy and deeper recovery to see them.

I finally submitted wholeheartedly to the process of emotional healing. It soon proved to be the best investment in myself that I could imagine. With it came the constant state and awareness of the fact that all life is inherently one, innocent, that God is its Creator, and all is well. To know that I was loved without conditions, I had to also love myself. This meant looking at and accepting the parts of me that I didn't want to previously. The gift is often where we fail to look.

We are aided on our path by devotion. Devotion bids us onward through the grind of being aware of where we fall short of unconditional love. We see that each condition that arises is a gift. We have tremendous faith in the compassion of God and we fall in love with "God's will be done." We do our best and accept that whatever happens is for the highest good. We pray to be a channel of God's peace, and we willingly surrender all to Him. We are always with Him and can rely on Him. With Him, we can forgive even the most horrendous situations. We don't always have to understand a situation in order to forgive it. When we lean on the Lord, an understanding will often suddenly arise and make the darkness illuminated, relieving us of unnecessary suffering.

It may require a little openness and effort to forgive, but the result is more than worth it. Deep down we desire to be free and we can be. Sometimes we just need someone to say, "Hey, this exists and you are worth it. Go this way because it's possible and good." I hope this little book can be such a pointer. You are very much worth the journey. Your role is important, and this world needs you. This I know.

CHAPTER 8
HUMOR

Whoever does not receive the Kingdom of God like a
little child will never enter it.[36]

The Path of Unconditional Love is the way of joy. "Let the little ones come unto me."[37] A tool of joy is humor. Joy spills over in all we do. We find ourselves easing others' burdens with our joy. This often takes the form of humor. We carry a lightness in our step, a melody in our way of being, and we bring a liveliness into our interactions. Juxtapose those with a suffering world. Love takes many forms.[38]

Humor helps lighten the load that we carry. There was a time when I was going through a deep struggle in my life. I went walking through a park with a feeling of trepidation. On the other

---

[36] Mark 10:15
[37] Matthew 19:14
[38] 1 Corinthian 9:19-23

side of the park was a bar so I went in and sat down. There was a younger man playfully teasing an older man across the bar. The old man sat expressionless, in sort of an apathetic way it seemed. It was apparent to me that the younger man was engaging with him from a place of love, even though it was slightly antagonistic banter. From watching this exchange, the giggles began to hit me hard. I couldn't hide the laughter. A spirit was felt to exude around the bar, it was tickling my insides. I left a different person, feeling free and renewed.

I was sitting with a friend before the blessed sacrament some years ago. It was just us two. We were quiet and in a devotional space. Suddenly, we both got swept up in a feeling of lightness. It seemed like we both started giggling simultaneously. We went on laughing for the next 15 minutes with the deepest and purest form of laughter one can feel. It came from joy. We were so relaxed and felt so much love that we just didn't move for some time. We received a blessing in that moment.

Humor often pushes boundaries and helps us expand our experience of being human. It helps us accept the difficulties that fall upon us. Laughter clears the way for seeing situations in a new perspective as it can lift the veil of our minds and reveal the beauty that was masked before.

Humor shows us that love speaks in a thousand tongues, but suffering is our option. We don't have to hold onto our sufferings as much as we would like to believe. Freedom comes from God, and God is present in our experience as love. Love is the opposite of suffering. There can be pain and love, but suffering and love are distinct. Suffering comes from our resistance to change. The obvious ease we feel through our joy reveals the absurdity that we think we can ever be separate from God's love.

We love our suffering! How can this be? We don't like to admit that, but it's part of the drama of our life that we become attached to. We identify with it and say, "Well, this is how it is." Our life is a reflection of what we hold to be true inside of us.

An interesting practice is to become observant of the mundane programs that pass through our heads during the day. Those programs are like an addiction, a repeating cycle of concepts that reflect back to us where we fall short of perfect love. When something doesn't go our way, what is our reaction? When someone says something about you that you don't agree with, how long do you ruminate on that? How quickly are we willing to accept the situation as it is and move on? Very few are those that have detached from the lure of these repetitive thought patterns. *We must decide to love God and our inner freedom more than we love our suffering and smallness in order to love without conditions.*

God's love for you knows no bounds. Those who come to know this love, who forgive and choose God above all else, carry an abundance of goodwill towards others. This is a reflection of grace in their life.

Love carries the intention to uplift others. This often happens on a level that is nonverbal. When others are sad, entrenched with negative programs, we can carry a soothing gaze towards them, an affirming validation of their being, and a warmth towards them that may help ease their load.

It is through the comedian that much of society is re-contextualized, accepted, and understood. Comedians often point out the pieces of society where our understanding is fuzzy and lacking clarity. It might be a sensitive area where society is still rigid, unforgiving, or entrenched with ignorant programming. The comedian will shed light on the confusion. There's a certain amount of daring and fearlessness that comes with this role, and a good deal of compassion.

Comedians are known as the "truth-sayers" traditionally. They can get away with speaking out about the darkened holes of society and placing them in a new light. They help us laugh at ourselves, which is extremely useful. Within that laughter is the release from the clutches of darkness. Aristotle was said to see comedy as "a purification of certain affections of our nature, not by terror and pity, but by laughter and ridicule".[39]

It is wise to not take yourself or your experience too seriously. On this path, we see accept that at any given moment we cannot see the totality of a situation. We're willing to give God the front seat and the final word. We know that the ultimate end is Peace. Peace comes from God. Therefore, we stay open to more information until we know peace.

---

[39] Rev. J.P. Mahaffy, "A History of Classical Greek Literature," London, 1895

When I experience myself in a funk, I notice one of the quickest ways out of it is by serving others. Confusion exists only in and because of the mind. It doesn't exist anywhere else. It's the experience of having a thinking mind. I notice the intention to bring a smile to others tends to bring a smile to me as well. Whatever baggage we are carrying with us, when the goodwill and laughter breaks through, it tends to exit rapidly.

Humor is that which grabs our attention and brings us out of the maze of our mind's thoughts, bringing us to a temporary completeness. This is why we love and pay high prices for viewing art. It's a temporary respite from our ills. It's a reset. Laughter does the same thing. We can't laugh and not be in the present moment. To laugh is simultaneously to surrender. With an escape, such as a movie, we repress what we are holding onto emotionally to deal with later. With laughter, there is an emotional release involved. We leave the situation altered, literally feeling "lighter".

Ever heard of the "fool for God"? It's a term that is more common in the Eastern Orthodox Church. It's been used to describe a person who is willing to be a servant to God in non-customary ways. God made us different, and in some servants, God expresses through them as comedy. A beautiful example of this is in the Russian made movie entitled "Ostrov", literally "The Island". The actor, Pyotr Mamonov, plays the role of the fool for God very believably. He is a man that the locals go to for answers and blessings. No one understands him, but they are blessed by him. He has been blessed by God and uses his gifts for others with unorthodox methods to get through to them. In the movie, he's found to be clucking like a chicken, barking like a dog, and making foolish seeming dances and gestures. All the while there is a deeper meaning and love behind what he does. He is being used as an instrument. It is compassion that fuels the "fool for God." And it is meant to bless.

The joyful cannot help but think of others. When love grows, an automatic consequence is to see yourself in others. It is not by volitional "trying" that this happens, it comes from a state of being. It is most perfectly exemplified in our society by the state known as Unconditional Love. One automatically is the servant of all, and it is one's joy to do so. It is what is "real" to the person of unconditional love as a state of being.

The joyful carry a kind of candor. People will often mistake joyful people for simpletons. However, the reverse is true. They've experienced the depths of life, accepted it, have forgiven it, and come out the other side. It is like they are carrying an ease about them. This ease is due to their security with their Higher Power, the one relationship that is forever and knows no bounds.

I once dated a woman who held a lot of trauma from childhood. When we would spend time with her mother, I saw myself be at my most comical. There was something sensed on some level that was a response to the burdensome feelings of their relationship together. Her mom must have felt I was such a clown, but I could not help it. To lighten the mood, the tone, and the feeling, I often came from a comedic angle. It felt important to help them laugh.

When I watch myself interact on social media, there is no "gain" I am seeking for. I am not seeking for anyone's approval, wanting to sell anything, or to convert anyone for some purpose. I interact from a space of joy and general goodwill towards life. What I feel as valid to post is that which is uplifting to others. There seems to be no other purpose for social media in my opinion.

Many people are driven by getting more money, success, sex, approval, etc. When these are stripped away, or eclipsed by a love for God, one finds a joyful innocence shining through. It is always there beneath our limited attitudes, intentions and desires.

I went through long periods of time where I felt the joyful expression that came through me needed to be quelled. I would post short, little dance videos from my time at gas stations, malls, or anywhere they were bold enough to play loud music. I would find myself posting deeply on love, sometimes several times a day when I had the time. It's hard to hide the strong feeling of love and inspiration. I realize that I likely appear strange to some acquaintances. It's hard to understand a person that is motivated by love, that which cannot be seen. Even the common religious can look at such expression in a skeptical manner.

After going back to my five-year college reunion, a friend told me that others were saying I was the "freak of the reunion." Ultimately, I came to see this as a compliment. "Well, it's evidence that perhaps this God-seeking is taking root," I giggled. I could not and would not resist the inspiration. When you find it, you realize that the riddles of life are not so complicated. That life is beautiful. This is what you've always sought for.

It is difficult to resist the "herd instinct", that which is considered normal and acceptable in society, the need to fit into this. It's especially so if the path you follow is exceptional. Much of what governs social behavior stems from the instinct to survive. This has been an important drive throughout human history. It's functionally beneficial because it will pull people up who are falling behind. However, the downside is that it will often try and suppress those who are not understood. As we look through the centuries, we see this happening to important geniuses in all fields, including Christianity. The ones that get a little ahead of what is commonly understood (ie., mystics).

To stand alone and follow God takes a lot of courage.[40] I am grateful that Jesus spoke about the resistance from society and that we would even be maligned for following Him. His words are inspiring and freeing. He taught me to always have courage, to not worry about the morrow, and to stand with the sword of truth.[41] When you feel God's grace and dedicate yourself to knowing Him more deeply, the inspiration is irresistible. This inspiration will likely pull you through any adversity that arises, even to the point of dying for Him.

---

[40] Luke 14:25-33
[41] John 15:20

When there is the absence of fear, we are free to be. This being, free of fear, is connected to a powerful, intuitive awareness that knows how to handle situations almost as if orchestrated. Because of this, love can express as comedy. Comedy and humor are often the best ways to slice through someone's defenses in order to connect with the dormant love inside them. Those who have followed me on social media for the last ten years can attest that my page is filled with an abundance of light-hearted comedy. There have been an abundance of dances and general, light-hearted goofiness in public. A feeling of inspiration will arise out of one's lovingness in the moment. This can be shared from the same joy and for no other reason than joy. However the world perceives us is irrelevant when we come from the completeness of joy. We are free to be the full expression of what we are. Let us be a light unto others. Let us be what we are.

CHAPTER 9
SURRENDER

Thy will be done.

Want to live an extraordinary life? Want to live with more freedom, peace, joy, security, and love? Want to be a blessing to the world? Here is the key: surrender. If there ever were a "secret" to living a life of true abundance, surrender is it.

Surrender is the hidden gem of Christianity, in my opinion. It is the core of our spirituality. However, it is not understood en masse. Most Christians have accepted Jesus into their heart, read the Bible, and attend church... and that's basically it. That kind of Christianity tends not to experience the deep fruits of the journey with Christ. There is a whole other world waiting for those who embark on this journey that I'm writing about in this book you are reading. It's difficult to describe, but the truly wise will not try to understand it necessarily. The truly wise will follow through on the path to becoming it. It's wide open and free. At the core of this path is surrender.

Surrender is the fulcrum by which we realize the presence of God. The fruits of this realization are beauty, love, joy, healing, peace, and all the things we ultimately yearn for. Surrender could be considered the core of all spirituality. We let go of the limited and open up to the unlimited. Spirituality essentially teaches various methods of surrender. We who are lost in the garden are surrendering to our Creator as the way out of suffering.

Surrender means to let go of, turn away from, remove, or no longer be a part of. The act of surrender is what frees us to be creative and spontaneous instruments for our loving God. It is through surrender that we become channels of peace. A phrase comes to mind: "Less of me, more of Thee."

If we are stuck in the past, it is hard to be of good use in this world. The moment is always ripe and new. It is we who do not see this, failing to be surrendered to the day.[42]

As a collegiate athlete who participated in American football, I was able to experience the effortless action of being totally surrendered in sports. I had prior experiences of being "in the zone", but the particular experience I am remembering now was beyond that. How the conditions were setup and this came to fruition I have no clue. However, to be completely surrendered was the result.

---

[42] Matthew 6:34

The game was on the line. I was feeling good. There was no stress, even though as a cornerback I was facing an All-American wide receiver who was much taller than me.

They were on their 20 yard line and needed to score to win the game. It was a '1 on 1' situation and the quarterback essentially threw the ball up in the air for his big receiver to go get it for the win.

I remember that time disappeared. This body was witnessed jumping in front of a receiver to make an interception. I was completely witnessing the whole thing. I jumped in front of him, saw the ball go into my hands, and started running down the field in the opposite direction. The depth of the surrender was to such an extent that I was completely aware that I was not doing it. And yet the body functioned and executed perfectly. That is the nature of surrender. When we are surrendered, we are relaxed, and we can execute in the world at higher levels than when trying to control life through our own means.

Although this experience lasted maybe 20 seconds temporally, it was an eternity, as all time disappeared. This was the greatest athletic feat I had ever been a part of. The play had won the game for our team. My family was in attendance and all were elated. However, I could take no pride in it, being fully aware that I didn't "do" it. I considered it a gift at the time. Little did I know of the full scope of what I had just experienced. It was a mystical state. I didn't tell anyone about it, as I didn't think anyone could understand. It was all witnessed.

❖

To be free, we must learn to surrender. If we are not prone to be willing to let things go, then we are prone to be in the way of the harmony that flows through life. Most humans live attached to things, people, situations, and events. Holding onto all that happens makes us a slave to sin. Our relationship with God is teaching us to be a slave to freedom instead.

Whether or when something is surrendered is not always in our personal control. So we take the necessary actions that we can to help set the conditions for the happening known as "surrender". For there to be surrender, we must have:

- a willingness to be self-reflective and look at what is not spiritually profitable
- a willingness to be devoted to love over all else
- a willingness to face and experience emotions
- the desire to be free
- a tremendous faith and trust in God's love for you

If there is a desire to be free, to be a channel of love, and to be a servant of the Lord, then the servant must be willing to say "yes" inwardly to limiting feelings and experiences. Jesus said "resist not evil" and when slapped to "offer the other cheek".[43] As you learn to surrender, you'll be able to lay down even your very life with complete acceptance out of love for God and truth.

The feeling may be apathy, anger, fear, desire, grief, pride, etc. There will be sensations experienced in the body along with these feelings. There may be a heaviness in the gut, a tightness in the chest, a burning feeling, or anything that is other than peace.

---

[43] Matthew 5:39

Pretend, for a second, that you just saw something that startled you and that you are carrying an anxious feeling. Instead of trying to wrestle with the feeling, notice your resistance to the feeling. Be willing to let go of the resistance and choose to feel it through instead. This practice will cause the feeling to disappear, where it can no longer influence your thoughts and actions. We habitually hold onto feelings for long periods of time, even for decades! That serves no one. To hold onto negativity is not spiritually profitable. That is why Jesus asks us to forgive. By practicing the art of surrender, you can be calm and collected in the moment instead of being controlled by a negative feeling.

Sometimes we feel we need to "pay" for our sins. That is God's job to decide on merits or demerits, not ours. You don't have the spiritual authority to choose punishment. Even God's word is: *I judge you not.*[44] Your job is to do your best every moment and *not* to wallow in shame, which ends up being a form of self punishment. God is peace, love and joy. Whatever is not peace, love or joy is not of God.

God does not punish us. However, our actions have consequences.[45] That is a law of life in this world. The best gift we can give the world is to have genuine remorse and to move onward, choosing better at the next opportunity. This may require making amends in the world if necessary and appropriate. The place where we are more apt to make positive change is when we

---

[44] John 8:15
[45] Luke 6:38; Galations 6:7

are not wallowing in guilt but courageously walking forward in love and compassion, holding the hand of Jesus.

The Process of Surrender: You can actually learn how to "haul away" debris that sits in your being. This debris can be repressed and play a factor in all you do throughout your life. To be free of this emotional debris is to feel lighter, more free and less ruled by things that limit your experience.

Decide to sit with a feeling that you want to be free of. What are you experiencing right now? Check your insides (your places of emotional feeling are generally in the abdomen and chest areas). Is there resistance, pain, or tightness? Instead of pushing it away to be dealt with later, can you allow the feeling now? Can you let it be here? Can you also let go of wanting to change the feeling? If you are able, inwardly allow the feeling to fully be what it is. Make a decision to no longer hold on to it. Stay with the feeling (not your thoughts about it). Let it be here, even choose it, and it will melt away. When your willingness to fully experience the feeling is at 100%, it will no longer be there and you'll feel lighter, more energetic and able in the moment.

Emotions are simply energy that has no business becoming stagnant. Stagnant energy creates physical, mental and spiritual suffering. That is how powerful our emotional energy is. We can repress and hold onto things for a lifetime. On some level, we think we are protecting ourselves by shielding ourselves from our emotions. However, the opposite is true. We are putting handcuffs on ourselves, limiting our experience.

This same process can be used with jealousy, regret, or fear. We can stop the inward resistance by getting out of our thoughts about it and by saying "yes" to whatever feeling that is arising. In this way, we are more free and we have better options placed before us. Our thoughts will always be colored by our internal world. That is why, as we submit to love, the options presented to us in thought are wider, better, and more holy in general. They will produce better fruit. Instead of dealing with something from a place of guilt, we can more effectively deal with the subject from a place of greater energy, i.e. love.

Upon awakening this morning, I had a throbbing headache. It was sufficiently strong that I would not want to write this paragraph or perform basic tasks. I sat down in my chair and looked at my resistance to the headache. I noticed the feelings of wanting to control it. I let go wanting to change anything about it. I could feel the resistance expand and a warmth and stillness take its place. Then a little more resistance bubbled up, so I allowed that to be here, treated it like a friend. Then I welcomed any remaining remnants of the headache, which was barely there at this point. Whatever strong feeling was there, I stopped resisting that. The headache seemed to move to the top of my head and then disappear. This example is true of a lot of our suffering. *We are choosing it.* And *keep choosing it.* The Master said, *"resist not evil"*. It is well with my soul.

❖

Trauma: Most of us are not in charge of our emotions because we don't know how to be. When things go well in life, we are fine. When difficulty arises, our emotional life crumbles. It seems the church is not really in the business of emotional healing and doesn't really know what to do with intense trauma. When is the last time people successfully dealt with underlying emotional trauma in church? It is rare. If you hang around any church member long enough, you'll see that they are carrying some form of trauma. In practice, it is easier to look like you are complete in your walk with Jesus than to actually hold up our broken pieces to a mirror and get honest about them.

One of the reasons trauma and deeper pain is not dealt with in churches is because there is not the field of unconditional love as a whole. That's a hard idea to swallow, but it is true. And likely this is because the path that Jesus taught is not stressed for us to follow in a devotional way, or as a realizable goal. What we can't do by ourselves becomes effortless due to the Presence of our Lord. The fruits of a church that is unconditionally loving are tremendous. It is a beacon of light and a healing balm to a suffering people. The energy of unconditional love is undeniable, and it sets the table for others to bring up the things they've kept hidden in the depth. With the field of unconditional love, it is ok to be who you are.

If your personal trauma is to be dealt with, you need to be heard. You need to be able to speak *from* those places of agony with complete acceptance of you and your experience. It is also wise to keep in mind: the healed become the healer for others. Others need your unconditional love as well. This will be the fruit of your experience. Your weakness becomes your strength.[46]

If we are to be healers of this world, as the Bible said we would[47], we must start with ourselves. We need to feel safe to reveal the pieces of ourselves that we have not yet accepted. As long as we see these parts of ourselves as "bad", we are judging ourselves and repressing our feelings.

It is time for the church to do the work begun by Jesus and the early followers of "the way". The torch was carried recently by St. Mother Teresa, but the baton is always available to be picked up. We begin by taking responsibility for ourselves. This is a holy work. The work of loving without conditions is the work of becoming healers for this world. Healing is an act of love. It is laying one's life down for others. We become healers through *surrendering to the Spirit of God*. We are unable to surrender what we haven't looked at within ourselves. So we have to get honest. This can be a tough path in the beginning, but in time, it becomes effortless. It is often initially difficult due to our resistance to feelings.

Surrender works because we are allowing God to do the work. God is "the Power" of this world. We are getting out of the way so He can do the work. What we can't do ourselves is effortless to God. How can we join with this effortless path? The answer is surrender.

---

[46] 2 Corinthians 12:9
[47] James 5:14-15

The modern day Christian has an opportunity to change the world. This will only happen by starting with oneself. Not by trying to force a world to see as we do. That's been done over and over. We need to carry the fruit of holiness! When we use force to convert others, we create an equal or greater counterforce. When we use the sweetness of a transformed and loving heart, it exudes a perfume that can't be denied and leaves a lasting effect on others. It cannot be pushed against because it doesn't want to change anyone. It leads by example and invitation, simply by being what it is. Holiness does the work by itself. Holiness comes from purity of intent, openness, honesty, forgiveness, surrender, faith, trust, and dedication. All these characteristics are magnified by our ability to love. Our ability to love is magnified tremendously by surrender.

The aim of this path is to be used by God as channels of His peace. Instead of coming from a mindset that we already know all that is, we humble ourselves, become empty, and ask our loving God to use us. What is Thy Will Lord? This is the path of the early Christians. What the followers of "The Way" did was empty themselves of everything. It is from this walk that immense power resides and from which blessings suffuse the entire world.

CHAPTER 10
EMOTIONS

Must needs offenses come, but woe from whom the offenses come.[48]

A stumbling block for many of us in the Christian sphere is our emotional life. We hold ourselves together, we play our part, we experience grace, we have a heart filled with charity... but, we are often unsure of how to deal with our emotional baggage and deep-rooted pain. This has been a big part of my personal journey, learning to heal and deal with the emotional landscape of my existence.

I come from a family plagued by generations of shame and guilt. Sprinkle in some alcoholism, and you get the picture. With this type of cycle, it seems evident that there is bound to be unaddressed trauma and pain.

---

[48] Luke 17:1

It is very common for us to repress our emotional pain. We are taught (especially men) to suck it up and move forward. In doing so, we leave something to be addressed at a later date, and this compiles upon itself. This will cause a person to not feel comfortable in their own skin and to likely feel alone, or that something is wrong with them. It seems evident that we do not have the knowledge or tools to deal with our emotional life in a healthy manner. We are taught how to read, write, and do math from a young age, but as far as our immediate experience with our complex emotional life, well… we're on our own!

There is a great fruit to be received in learning to navigate a healthy emotional life. It is our gift to ourselves, our family, and our future generations. We live in a time where this can now be readily addressed.

Let me tell you a little of my story: I became very inspired to serve God during my college years. For the first time in my life, I would feel joy bubble up. However, just around the bend, it seemed there was always a heaviness about to arise, a depressive weight. I didn't know what to do about this. I was even embarrassed about it. I thought if I just prayed a little harder or was blessed a little more, it might go away on its own. Turns out these things don't go away until they are addressed and healed.

I also found that deep emotional weight or trauma cannot be addressed alone. We need the help of others to support us because the energy of the trauma itself is sufficiently low enough that we don't have the strength or energy to face it and heal by ourselves. To try and do so means to lean on the same energy of the problem to face the problem, which adds to the problem. The problem can only be addressed appropriately from a place that has the requisite energy to heal the problem, for example, unconditional love.

When I decided to "be in" my body and experience my emotions, I noticed that I had cut myself off from having to feel them. This was likely due to traumatic experiences in childhood. I thought I was feeling them, but when I scanned my body in association with a feeling, I noticed I wasn't actually feeling the emotion inside of me. I was feeling mainly in my mind.

There is always a feeling inside our body that correlates with an emotion. I could emotionally feel in my heart area (in the middle of my chest), but there was a tremendous pain there that went along with that opening of feeling. This pain took seven years to resolve. There was a point where I made the resolve, "I'm going to go into my feelings, and feel them... no matter what it takes." I no longer wanted to be cut off from them.

For two straight weeks, whenever I had spare time, I would put my awareness inside of my body. At first, it was like touching electricity. It was so intense that I probably averaged around two hours of sleep per night. But ultimately, it was more than worth it. What came through on the other side of this experience was a deeper freedom and depth to life. I felt uplifted and extremely joyful. It was like a return to my true being. I was doing all this as a servant of Lord Jesus.

The pain in the heart region continued, however. It was torturous. I was also in some dysfunctional relationships at the time. I couldn't understand why this was happening to me. I was striving hard to serve the Kingdom, yet I was attracting relationships where my partners would neglect my experience and feelings. I was attracting wounded souls to fulfill the unconscious roles I was choosing from my repressed pain.

I finally broke down and began a quest. Soon thereafter, I found answers in a 12-step program. I went to *Adult Children of Alcoholics*. It was then I started to realize the emotional baggage I had been lugging around. This part of me wanted to be known. With the help of others in the program, where I felt loved and safe, I was able to reveal the inner workings of my pain. Six times in the first half year in the program I experienced releases of trauma. Essentially, something would come to mind from childhood and I would have a deep cry. I let myself be vulnerable in front of all my newfound friends in the program. To heal can take tenacity. The program allowed a safe space to explore myself, to let out what needed to come out. We do this out of love for ourselves.

Once these emotional issues were addressed, with the help of the Steps and some program-recommended one-on-one counseling, there wasn't a darkness left waiting to color my experience anymore. There wasn't a "victim" ploy (me being a victim to this emotional baggage). I became emotionally reliable and balanced all the time. I now had the open road to love without conditions.

Each of us carries something called a *shadow*. It consists of the disowned pieces of ourselves that we would rather not face. For many of us, there is tremendous fear in approaching it. Much of the shadow exists due to lies we have told ourselves. And because of these lies, we feel unlovable. In truth, nothing about us is unlovable.

We have always done our best. Our "best" changes from day to day, and moment to moment. In one moment we are not in the same place physically, mentally, and spiritually as we are in another moment. We are beset by numerous difficulties in life. It's not easy for a single human being.

Through the practice of forgiveness, I have found that the only judgement in the world is the judgement in my own mind. I am responsible for the thoughts that run through my mind, no one else's. Any seeming judgement outside of my mind is non-existent. We all see through our own programs, and most of these were imposed upon us without our realizing it. Those that judge see life through a lens of pain, which is their shadow unconsciously running in the background, coloring experience. Our own being pays the price for this. None of us can claim to see truth at any given time. Therefore, we see through an act of perception. When our shadow is owned, we float a little higher and the way we relate to life is more easy-going and in love. When our stored emotional baggage has been healed sufficiently, love more effortlessly becomes a way of being. We see the innocence and lovability in others because we are in touch with the same innocence that we are.

The idea of what love "is not" should have likely been addressed earlier in this book; let's do so now. Love is not "dogooderism". Love is not the deed, in itself. It may express as deeds, but it stems from being loving. Love isn't necessarily something of form, something we can always see and point to. Love is a way of being. It's a conscious connection and unity felt with life. We do what we do as a consequence of seeing the same life in others.[49] Not because we "should", for that is not love. Love isn't about moralism or doing good deeds to be seen as good. Good deeds tend to happen through the loving, and the deeds are not even considered. The deeds are a reflection. Goodness is what we are because God is our Source and we have been given the gift of life. Love is the result of a closeness with God when the limiting blocks of human perception are healed. Love is present when we allow ourselves to be free from the control of that which is not love.

How do we allow the Holy Spirit to work through us? Through this holy path of love, we submit our will to the Lord. If we are in the way of our Lord, the translation of His Word through us can become blurry and mixed up. The way of God is the way of light. We make way for the Lord. Our body is our house, and we keep it picked up and clean. We always keep a fire burning and a warm place for our tender Lord Jesus to rest his feet.

Today's Christianity could be said to be watered down by some. If we look at what following Jesus meant to the early Christians, they surrendered wholeheartedly. They were utterly

---

[49] Luke 6:45

convinced that Jesus is Lord and knew what this meant. This is our Lord instructing us! What could be more important?

The early Christians did not change Christ to suit their political or philosophical ends. They looked to and sought direction from the Lord only. We sometimes try hard, but have we lost the vision and core of what it means to follow Jesus? Does following Jesus equate to words in a book? No, it never could. If it did, Jesus would not have upbraided the pharisees. The Law must be written in our hearts.[50] Let God write His Word in our hearts and minds. We strive hard for religion, but religion is simply an imperfect vessel made by men to worship God. It's a ship directed to the Lord but guided by mankind. I love the Church! But I don't mistake it for Jesus. If I want to know Jesus, I'll find him only where he actually is.

Few are they that heal the sick and lame, raise the dead, and feed the multitude. And yet, there is as much of God present with us as there was with the disciples. There can never be "less of God." There can only be those of lesser faith, or those who "err", those that have not realized the profundity of a relationship with our Father in Heaven.

Which is more important, the heart of an enterprise or its appearance… the inside or the surface? Experience has shown me that there is more integrity in being the change within ourselves before we seek to enact this change in the world. As a young man, I was once told "it's what you are that matters most, not what you do." I didn't like this at first because it meant that I actually had to

---

[50] Jeremiah 31:33

conform and change to adhere to God's will... and not the other way around. I wanted to be great and act of my own will and ideas, instead of wanting to be small and surrendered for my Lord's use. *Holiness is the path of becoming lesser for the sake of the greater.*

The church needs holiness, not do-gooders, if it is to thrive and prosper. That which doesn't come from true holiness ultimately divides, no matter how clever. A house cannot stand long without a solid foundation. Intimacy and identity with Christ is that foundation. The church needs people yearning to enter into the inner sanctum of a spiritual life with Christ. This is what gives validity to our faith, and from it, fountains of blessings. If this book meets one person and inspires them to pursue an intimate relationship with Christ through devotion, humility, and surrender, then I am eternally grateful. The suffering of the world is lessened because of this one thing, and the purpose of life is afoot for the individual.

The most poignant cinematic scene of Jesus, for me, is from the movie "Jesus of Nazareth"[51]. Jesus (portrayed by actor Robert Powell) chastises the supposed 'holy people' of the time. He says: "Woe to you scribes and pharisees. Hypocrites all! For you shut up the kingdom of Heaven against men. You do not go in yourselves, nor do you let others enter. Blind guides!"[52] May we be the ones on the right side of history. Those who enter the Kingdom and invite others. Not those that do the seemingly right things, but fail to enter.

---

[51] *Jesus of Nazareth* 1977. Zefferelli.
[52] Matthew 23:13

St. Peter will likely not meet you at the gates of heaven and say, "Good job, you chose the right belief system[53]... you're in!". More likely, this moment of truth will reveal what lies in our hearts, the truth of what we are and how we led our life.[54] What is your essence? What is the truth about you? Do you realize that everything about you is already known?[55] Do you love God with all your heart, mind, and soul?

Being loving does not mean being walked on. One can stand for truth with strength, when necessary, while being unconditionally loving and anchored in God. Much like there are times as a parent that the highest form of love is to discipline a child.

In walking the 12-step circles I learned about *codependency*. Essentially, that's putting other peoples opinion, experience, and needs above our own. We learn it in childhood, perhaps from the wanting of approval from a parent that doesn't give it (the literal passing of emotional wounds from one generation to another). We alter our behavior to try and win the affection we so desperately feel we need. We can't help but feel like our wellbeing depends on it.

---

[53] Matthew 7:7
[54] 1 Peter 3:3
[55] Matthew 10:29

If we are codependents, we cannot stand for truth very easily, or without making a hassle about it, as it feels like betraying something sacred. Wanting another's approval can mean more to us than our own feelings even. Our emotions tell us we need this person's approval in order to survive. But that is a lie. Others cannot give us what we can only receive from God in our own soul. These are the types of emotional issues that a servant of Christ needs to walk through if one should be an expression of Christ's love on this earth.

One gift of the path of loving without conditions is that it helps lead to discernment. Discernment arises when we have filtered out the emotional presuppositions and programs of the mind sufficiently. Discernment helps us to see what is ephemeral and what is eternal. What is real and what is false. What matters and what is irrelevant. We increasingly rely on God for our understanding of the world, and this happens through an intuitive type of knowing and connection with God. It becomes a way of being and how we operate. You can look down the street and get the essence of a stranger or situation instantly because we are relying on God.

Instead of living in fear of emotions, we can learn to welcome them. Emotions are not an enemy. They are simply the feedback of our human experience. The fastest route to peace in any situation is to surrender to God. We surrender the outlook, the feelings, the ideas... everything. To know the peace of God is to align with the Spirit of Christ.[56] We will fall down but we continually rise up. We don't expect perfection, but we are open to progress. We turn everything over to God.

Of course you have spiritual gifts. These normally come out of hiding when we are filled with inspiration from the Lord. The inspiration of our Lord expresses as the Grace to want to know Him. Through the path of Christ, our gifts are revealed. St. Paul once said that if we have not love, we are as a noisy gong or clanging cymbal. It is the same with our spiritual gifts... If we have not love, they are worthless. Therefore, do not pray for them; rather, pray to be like Christ in love. Upon that foundation the spiritual gifts have greater meaning and a more powerful effect in the world. We must be selfless to be entrusted with gifts, otherwise our limitation can get in the way and cause harm. All glory is due to God.

---

[56] Philipians 4:6

CHAPTER 11
CONTEMPLATION

Could you not keep watch with me for one hour?[57]

When intending to follow the teaching of Christ, it is wise to know a few simple prayers that encompass the Spirit of Christ. When all else fails, we lean on scripture and prayer for direction and assistance.

These prayers can be contemplated line by line, or said as a whole. We might open up to a phrase while simultaneously opening up to the Lord. The inner portion might be, "what is this Lord? What would you have me know about this? Teach me, Lord." We ask the Lord to reveal their deeper meaning to us. These lines are pregnant with much fruit to help aid us on the path towards loving without conditions.

---

[57] Matthew 26:40

The Prayer of St. Francis

Lord, make me an instrument of your peace:
where there is hatred, let me sow love;
where there is injury, pardon;
where there is doubt, faith;
where there is despair, hope;
where there is darkness, light;
where there is sadness, joy.

O divine Master, grant that I may not so much seek
to be consoled as to console,
to be understood as to understand,
to be loved as to love.
For it is in giving that we receive,
it is in pardoning that we are pardoned,
and it is in dying that we are born to eternal life.

Amen.

The Lord's Prayer

Our Father, who art in heaven,
hallowed be thy name;
thy kingdom come;
thy will be done;
on earth as it is in heaven.
Give us this day our daily bread.
And forgive us our trespasses,
as we forgive those who trespass against us.
And lead us not into temptation;

but deliver us from evil.
For thine is the kingdom,
the power and the glory,
for ever and ever.

Amen.

The Serenity Prayer

God, grant me the serenity
to accept the things I cannot change,
the courage to change the things I can,
and the wisdom to know the difference.

Living one day at a time,
enjoying one moment at a time;
accepting hardship as a pathway to peace;
taking, as Jesus did,
this sinful world as it is,
not as I would have it;
trusting that You will make all things right
if I surrender to Your will;
so that I may be reasonably happy in this life
and supremely happy with You forever in the next.

Amen.

Reinhold Niebuhr

Psalm 91

Whoever dwells in the shelter of the Most High will rest in the shadow of the Almighty. I will say of the Lord, "He is my refuge and my fortress, my God, in whom I trust." Surely he will save you from the fowler's snare and from the deadly pestilence. He will cover you with his feathers, and under his wings you will find refuge; his faithfulness will be your shield and rampart. You will not fear the terror of night, nor the arrow that flies by day, nor the pestilence that stalks in the darkness, nor the plague that destroys at midday. A thousand may fall at your side, ten thousand at your right hand, but it will not come near you. You will only observe with your eyes and see the punishment of the wicked.

If you say, "The Lord is my refuge," and you make the Most High your dwelling, no harm will overtake you, no disaster will come near your tent. For he will command his angels concerning you to guard you in all your ways; they will lift you up in their hands, so that you will not strike your foot against a stone. You will tread on the lion and the cobra; you will trample the great lion and the serpent. "Because he loves me," says the Lord, "I will rescue him; I will protect him, for he acknowledges my name. He will call on me, and I will answer him; I will be with him in trouble, I will deliver him and honor him. With long life I will satisfy him and show him my salvation."

Anyway

People are often unreasonable, irrational, and self-centered.
Forgive them anyway.
If you are kind, people may accuse you of selfish, ulterior motives.
Be kind anyway.
If you are successful, you will win some unfaithful friends and some genuine enemies.
Succeed anyway.
If you are honest and sincere people may deceive you.
Be honest and sincere anyway.
What you spend years creating, others could destroy overnight.
Create anyway.
If you find serenity and happiness, some may be jealous.
Be happy anyway.
The good you do today, will often be forgotten.
Do good anyway.
Give the best you have, and it will never be enough.
Give your best anyway.
In the final analysis, it is between you and God.
It was never between you and them anyway.

Mother Teresa

Christ Be With Me

Christ with me, Christ before me
Christ behind me, Christ in me
Christ beneath me, Christ above me
Christ on my right, Christ on my left
Christ when I lie down, Christ when I sit down
Christ when I arise, Christ to shield me
Christ in the heart of everyone who thinks of me
Christ in the mouth of everyone who speaks of me

St. Patrick

When we contemplate these prayers, we align our life with the teaching of Christ, which is to be unconditionally loving. This way of being is very powerful as an expression in the world. It is a gift to humanity. Whereas most of the things we can do in the world have some form of limitation, this path gives to the world *silently and unendingly*. It nurtures all life from within. We must seek to abide with His Spirit, that we may be that gift to the world.

Quiet Contemplation

Inward prayer is most powerful and important. This type of prayer goes on throughout our day. We "spend time with" the words and allow them to transform our being. This can be called *contemplative prayer*. Many of us vocally pray, and then we go back to the repetitious words and habits of our mind world. With contemplation, we are, in a way, chiseling away at the hypnotism from the world so that we may see through the eyes of Christ.

Heartfelt prayer can lead to an inner stillness with the Lord. This type of prayer has been called by many names through the centuries: secret place of the most high, prayer of quiet, cloud of unknowing, practicing the presence of God, centering prayer, or simply meditation. The ultimate aim of this kind of prayer is to sit with God in Silence, inwardly quiet.

The most intimate communication one can have is before God in holy silence. Words are limited and God does not need them.[58] The greatest prayer we can give for the world is to be with God's Holy Presence, humble and quiet. The mind is in repose and the heart is at ease. At first, it may seem difficult to be with God in this way. But in time, it not only becomes natural but can become a part of our every day living. We need not strive for what is always with us. However, the mind may rebel. Forgive the mind, it doesn't know any better. All it knows is to think it has to paddle, paddle, paddle... paying no attention to the fact that the river is already flowing beneath us. God makes the rivers flow, and He will take us where He wants us to be.

To be with, hang out with, and surrender to God is to live in prayer.[59] There is not a more powerful form of prayer. One cannot exactly tell you what the presence of God is, that must be found by you alone. It can only be pointed to. It is surely not the clanking of the mind. Nor is it encompassed by thought. In your highest moments in prayer, be aware of the warm and silent place. Surrender to this place like a child to their mother's chest. Avoid

---

[58] Matthew 6:8
[59] 1 Thessalonians 5:16

thoughts if you can, only abide in silence. Ask God to reveal his Presence to you and set yourself aside.

This path is asking you to love God more than anything in this world, even your own thoughts. Does this seem radical? It may at this point in your journey, and that is ok. Not everyone is ready for this type of communion with God. However, it will present itself to the lover of Christ that is ready. After all, God is our Source, and our ultimate end. Should we not put Him above all else? Because we put Him first, we love all life. We perform our tasks with a clear mind and an open heart.

Simplicity

As we reform our being to adhere to God's laws and ways, the outward appearance is one of simplicity. As a matter of fact, life does become simpler, both inside and out. Our purpose is known. Our direction is certain. The meaning of life is clear.

The depths of this simplicity are understood by few. However, when the world is lacking, this simplicity transforms into immense strength. What is lacking is fulfilled. There is an inner hidden reservoir of power and strength that comes from this love. With never-ending energy and zest, this silence and simplicity are transformed into a thunderous roar.

CHAPTER 12
REMINDERS

Let not steadfast love and faithfulness forsake you; bind them around your neck; write them on the tablet of your heart. So you will find favor and good success in the sight of God and man.[60]

You are loved beyond what you could ever know. If life appears hard, there's a purpose even to that. The purpose may be to help eschew what is in the way of something greater. Be willing to see it through to the other side and never lose sight that love is the prerequisite of existence. There could be no love without God, and no God without love. They are forever intertwined. You can rely on that 100%.[61]

Do not rely on appearances solely. What the mind perceives unaided can be misleading. With humility, the greatest intellects

---

[60] Proverbs 3:3-4
[61] John 4:16

shine brightest. So it is with spirituality. When we are humble and allow Providence her due chance, we have much greater options at our behest. Include God in the equation. Lean on that always.

Do not compare yourself to others. It is fruitless and pointless. The subtleties of your being cannot be fathomed. They are unique to every individual, as are each individual's fruits. Why God made you as He did was not to be compared to the appearance of another. Be your greatest expression. That it may shine brightly upon a sleeping world.[62]

Never lose sight of your goal. Let it be a part of your life as you would the air you breathe. Take one prayer or spiritual goal and become that. This is a life well-lived.

When there is spiritual growth, challenges can arise. See them as opportunities. Be mindful. Be resolute. Don't stray from basic spiritual principles. This is the humble path of love by which we give God all honor.

---

[62] Matthew 5:15-16

Spiritual gifts can arise for the seriously devoted. Realize that we must be a steward of such gifts. When I was young and devoted, I had no one there to warn me. Thankfully, there was the intuition to not claim credit or take them personally. To do so is spiritual error. At best, we have been given a gift for which we are a steward. All glory be to God.

God is a friend to those in need. With whatever is lacking, go to God first. God is the storehouse of power and abundance, as all comes from Him. Jesus said to the woman at the well, "whoever drinks of the water I will give him, will never be thirsty again."

Should you endeavor on Jesus' path, you might be misunderstood by many, perhaps most, in your life.[63] Accept it now. That way you will not be tempted to hold a grievance when it happens. Most people are hypnotized by this world and its appearances. Most people are living for temporary gains. That's ok. That's their perfection at this time. Allow others to have their experience, forgive whatever appears. Do not stray from what is important. Jesus needs you, if He is to be Him. We are His instruments. You are part of the plan He brought to us.

---

[63] Matthew 10:35

When you are on your deathbed, what kind of life do you want to be responsible for living? In giving God everything now, there will be no surprises at death. Only a grateful welcoming. For surely, nothing was ever yours while on earth.

A major stumbling block to the heart opening (literally opening to the spirit of love) is one's reliance on the mind's perception as the only "real". The mind that thinks it knows limits itself to its own understanding and falls short. With the inclusion of the heart, a greater context of perception arises. The great healers and saints throughout time brought a fresh vision and were able to uplift others by their extraordinary hearts.

The mind has given humanity great advances in science, but it is the heart that gives life meaning. Without love, we still are only living a limited existence. Through love, we are inspired to lay down even our life for truth.

It is a gift to have an open heart in a world of sleeping people. The heart is where our greatest strength comes. When all else looks dire, the heart believes. The heart pulls down the power of God and infiltrates the places nothing and no one else can. The heart lives for everyone. The loving see themselves in others. The loving remind us who we are.

Heartfelt music has a powerful effect on listeners. When leadership is from the heart, it energizes the heart in others. We learn the deepest lessons of life when we are called to sacrifice ourselves for others. We are all leaders and teachers for others. Dedication of love for family, for country and for God is inspirational for all time.

Where there is no humility, there is no God. Obviously, God is Omnipresent, but where the human lacks humility, the presence of God acting through the human falls short. Humility is not something one can acquire like an object bought at a store. It's something that comes about in time, of its own accord, through wisdom.

There are two earmarks of a close relationship to God: joy and humility. Joy is natural and is part of our everyday life. If it has not been discovered yet... keep going. Joy will not be there, or will be short lived, if there is not humility. Humility does not say, "Oh, I'm lesser than thou." True humility comes from honesty and an accurate assessment of what one is.

The mind is seen as the tool that it is, of great benefit to the altering things in the material world but limited in scope and its ability to see the total picture of any given situation. This kind of humility is found when the avenue's of self will have been exacerbated. In the 12-step programs, they call this "hitting rock bottom". A deep surrender often comes out of the ashes of despair. When we have nowhere else to turn, we are more apt to let go. God is found to be on the other side. All along, what was standing in the way was our own mind's pride. The need to have it "our way".

If we still believe our thinking to be something magical and amazing, we are ultimately in for a rude awakening. At some point, the mind lays down its pride and sees the futility of trying to understand and manipulate symbols (words and concepts) to attempt to grasp what is ungraspable. The Absolute (God) is known by identity through relationship, not by mental strength. Peace is found when we let go of that which stands in the way of knowing God.

Everything that happens to us here on earth is an opportunity. EVERYTHING. It might be an opportunity to surrender to God and to accept His Will. It might be an opportunity to forgive. It could be an opportunity to let go of control, to be honest, or to choose for love. There is nothing that happens here that is not utilized on the path of loving without conditions. And that is why this path carries with it the epitome of meaning and purpose. It leads to the great understanding of life: *love is the ultimate law*. This truth can only be found by surrendering to it.

Lastly, be strong. Be courageous. Believe with all your heart. Never give up. Always strive for what is good. Keep a compassionate heart. If you are strong with a tender heart, you will be like a magnet and bring many towards God. God will never leave you unaided, even though it might feel like it at times. God cannot leave His own unaided. We must be patient and loyal.

CHAPTER 13
PITFALLS

*For the gate is narrow and the way is hard that leads
to life, and those who find it are few.*[64]

It is possible to lose all the momentum one has gained on this
path due to lack of experience or not being forewarned of the
pitfalls that lay in wait for us. There is that which opposes us
because of our growing closeness to the Lord. Many beings deny
the reality of God, and they will deny, mock, and try and knock
you down at times. We need grace to grow in this life. To fall
down in this life, we only need a human mind that is blind to
temptation.

Let me be clear about discerning what is good and what is not.
It's actually very simple: *follow that which leads to the Lord, and
avoid that which doesn't.* Many things will be presented to you in

---

[64] Matthew 7:14

all your openness and innocence. In the beginning, it's sometimes hard to tell the difference. As you become more seasoned it becomes more clear.

There is beauty from all cultures on this earth. There is also that which can lead one astray. There are 10,000 ideas on how to live aright. There are also 10,000 ideas on how to seek God. A simple rule of discernment can be the point upon where you ask yourself: *does this help me love and serve Christ the more?* If the answer is "no", then consider not wasting your precious energy.

There is no human head above your own. It doesn't matter how holy appearing another person seems to be, they are still human and beset with the same limitations that all of us are. The only difference is that some have trodden the path of surrender for a longer period of time. For this, we feel gratitude and learn what we can while never forgetting that the Lord shines equally upon all who ask.

In some circles, this has been forgotten and people have been placed on pedestals. Large sums of money have been given to teachers, teachings, and organizations that do not represent truth. Most often people are ensnared by their desire for the spectacular. God is the storehouse of all Grace! No mortal is.

Nothing brings me greater joy than others falling in love with the Lord. It is the home of all homes. It is our destiny. Our final resting place. And rest it is, even when we are in action. As a young seeker, there were a few things I wish I had known from the start. Much of the new age movement is false. There might be some well-intentioned and loving people that we could classify as new age, but for the most part, it's filled with diversions. They sometimes sound legitimate, so it can be confusing. These will often involve people channeling and doing something close to magic and all kinds of unnecessary practices. Avoid these traps at all costs.

When my heart first opened up to the Lord's inspiration, I was beguiled by a smart sounding New Age teaching. It seemed like it could possibly be true. You see, my ability of discernment was infantile. I was naive and impressionable. I remember sharing some of what I learned with another young man. That teaching "felt good" to me then. What was more, he seemed influenced by it. It's like I had some charisma at that time, being newly open to the Lord and so excited to learn. Shortly thereafter, I had the benefit of seeing through the ignorance of my ways. My heart ached for that young man. I got down on my knees and prayed for him with tears many times. Ever since I have begged the Lord to never let me lead a soul astray with anything false. It is so painful to think that can happen. Lord, please protect this writer from the deleterious, and Lord, please protect the reader from the deleterious. May they be blessed and protected by the Lord, filled with love and righteousness.

The young seeker of God has their heart and mind open. This is a beautiful thing to behold. It is also a time that needs some caution. The seeker is not yet adept at seeing the limitations and pitfalls around them. Traps will be set. There are times when everything does appear to be love. God's grace can be felt everywhere. The innocence and lovability of others shines through. Even miracles happen. It's also important that a servant be made aware of the temptations and challenges that will arise. That which does not want you to progress on this planet will come out to tempt you. It will be cloaked in something seemingly innocent. It will try to ensnare you and knock you off the path. It could use vanity, sexual seduction, power, money, and even some forms of spiritual attack are possible.

This path is more important than can be put into words because each time a soul commits to the Lord and follows the path of perfecting oneself to loving without conditions, that which is evil is exposed and threatened in the process. We are all fallen, by default. To be born a human is to be born into sin, literally to see in "error". That sin is to believe we are separate from God, and thus every action and thought has selfishness at its root. We try to live separate from and without God, usurping his Majesty. This is what leads to misery.

We are a part of the mission of Jesus Christ. We become a part of His mission by saying "yes" to Him. Following Christ transforms the human soul into agents of beauty and love. We are choosing not for our sinful nature, but for Spirit, Light, and Truth (aspects of God). When our being is transformed, so is the world we see. There is no better investment one could make for oneself, and no better gift one could give the world. We lovers of Christ set patterns for others to follow. We say "yes" to that which leads to God.

Pride does in fact blind us. We get spiritually sluggish and do not want to change. We become blind to our own ignorance and lack of conformity to God's world. This is when we become entrapped by the thinking of the world and the limited mind, which when unaided, is not aligned with peace and love. The egoic mind wants to dominate, be in control, manipulate, and be free of any consequences. However, there are consequences to everything we choose.[65]

I highly recommend the 12 steps to deal with the addictions or trauma you may have. I know many people suffer silently and are not sure how to get help. I wanted to share a little of my experience with the steps and how I benefitted.

I was raised in a family with some hidden alcoholism in its wake. When I grew willing to deal with some childhood trauma I joined a 12-step program called *Adult Children of Alcoholics*. It was transformative for me. It was the first time I had been validated and seen in areas I was ailing. It's a safe space of acceptance where we are anonymous (no one speaks of members by name outside of the meetings).

---

[65] Luke 6:38

There are 12-step groups for addictions to lust (pornography), narcotics, alcohol, partners of alcoholics, codependents, debtors, food addiction, gamblers, emotions, sex and love addiction, workaholism, and the list goes on. These groups are a backbone to our society, transforming untold numbers of people's lives. Groups are available worldwide.

I personally went through around 6 trauma releases in the first 6 months of my exposure to the steps. I needed to be heard, seen, and understood. I found nothing but compassion and love from the group of people who became part of my spiritual family.

I have written about the steps here because it is a safe space to heal from difficult areas in our life where our church and family are likely unable to address these needs properly. It is a place where we are accepted, heard, and loved. The core of the steps, in my experience, is honesty and surrender.

I would love to one day see a 12-step group called "ASOUL", Anonymous Servants Of Unconditional Love". A safe place to share the journey of loving without conditions. The steps themselves, discovered through Bill Wilson in the late 1930s to help himself and others overcome alcohol addiction, are a huge blessing to society. They help further the mission of Lord Jesus Christ, even unbeknownst to its practitioners. Many an atheist is transformed into a God loving soul. That is the power of spiritually-based programs.

Stay clear from most every New Age idea. The concepts in this arena are ploys to maintain a desirous mind and "special" personal identity. However, the mind is beguiled because some concepts seem "spiritual". That is an easy place for confusion, when there is in fact a grain of truth in the product. For instance, the idea of "manifesting" is a dead end. It's a carrot for the the young aspirant who is desirous of "stuff". You go down that rabbit hole and eventually you'll realize you've been hoodwinked, but not until you've spent tons of money on books, seminars, and life coaches who charge large amounts to teach you how to do this. You will get more from this simple path than all of those "extraordinary" sources combined.

There are times when one can hear helpful words and intuitive knowing from angels, God's helpers. However, channeling is something different. The channeler is literally giving over their consciousness to another entity who they really know nothing about. We are here to learn and grow, not to be codependent with lost spirits that for some reason have an interest in life here on earth. Many of them are truly outlandish and dangerous. Whatever needs to be known was said by Christ. Don't waste time in New Age diversions.

What you garner on the path of unconditional love is yours forever. It will enhance all aspects of your life. Do not stray from it. Keep this goal in mind every day and in due time you'll have made good progress. There is no greater gift to yourself.

If the teaching doesn't put God first, if it tries to make *you* into something powerful and special, then it's playing with your ego and it's a dead end. The acronym for ego is said to be "edging God out". Healthy self-esteem is one thing, that will come naturally on this path, but claiming power separate from God is sheer nonsense. There is only one power in this life, it is what created us. The access we have to it is by alignment with it. All else is false.

CHAPTER 14
DAILY LIFE

All Scripture is inspired by God and profitable for teaching, for reproof, for correction, for training in righteousness.[66]

What does daily living on this path look like? To each their own, however, a few things are likely common to most.

1. We take time for prayer and meditation in the morning. This sets the whole day aright. The purpose of prayer and meditation is to open ourselves up to God, to be fed by Him directly, to listen, and to carry this connection with us throughout our day in all we do.

2. We examine our conscience daily. Where did I fall short today? What could I do better? We acknowledge our limitations and ask for help doing better in the future.

---

[66] 2 Timothy 3:16

3. We ask for help and assistance to do God's bidding on earth.

4. We pray silently for others throughout the day.

5. We accept being small, as opposed to the need for being special, seen, heard, praised, etc. We must be ok being no one so that God might be bigger in our experience.

6. We carry the intention to see the beauty of others.

7. We look to God in all circumstances.

8. We are watchful of our desires.

9. We are honest.

10. We find our joy in Heaven. There is a lessening attraction to the things of the world.

11. We are disciplined because we know that time is short here.

12. We are grateful because every day is better, even if there are hard days. We go through it all for love.

It has been natural for me to carve out a space to sit and "be with God" every morning. I put that in quotes simply because we can never not be with God. Having a space dedicated to just sitting and be prayerful, contemplative and meditative helps fuel the intention to be unconditionally loving due to the energy of devotion. When one enters this domain in their house, it is very likely their mind will turn to God.

You might have inspirational photos, books, or even candles and incense. I have preset playlists of music, such as Gregorian chant, that I play each morning. I normally have photos of Jesus, Mary, and the saints to gaze at. They are merely tools, but I look up to each one of them for the gift of their life. It is wise to keep a few books close to you that were written by others who have trodden the path of Christ. This becomes motivational for your own experience.

Your space often becomes an outpouring of what is inside you. Make your space beautiful to you so that you will feel inspired there. When you sit in the morning, consider the idea of not starting your day until you've given your "first fruits" to God and feel a connection to Him. This connection may come in silence.

The ultimate goal of your devotion is not that it becomes a thing you do from time to time, but that it becomes a way of life. We come to realize that we are always before the Lord, so we are humble, loving, gentle, open, giving, and joyful out of gratitude for the love that is life.

You are loved and beautiful. As you go about your day, love will naturally and spontaneously sprout in your experience. The more we let go of our ignorance, the more we can see the truth clearly: God is love, and His love is for one and all.

Many will be blind to God's love. Who cares? We can still love our Creator through them. You don't have to agree with the thought programs of an individual, there is something there to love regardless.

The same life that is in you is in all. Different expressions, but all souls point to God's handiwork as Creator. Jesus is there[67] (see Mother Teresa's prayer, "Anyways"). By our free will, many have

---

[67] Matthew 25:40

chosen to be blind to this fact. And that is ok. I trust in God and I trust in His Salvation. I needn't fight life or try and prove others wrong. I can trust Him to take care of what needs to be done, making me aware of what needs to be made aware of. I am a willing and faithful servant. That is all.

People can be blown away by the intense energy of love when expressed through others. I remember needing to learn how to navigate the loving energy I felt and how that might translate to more complete or balanced interactions with others. People can misperceive what that lovingness means and mistake it as personal attraction. Some people are so cut off from love that they see it as unreal.

As the lovingness matures, it's transformed into a more calm way of being. It can transform into being present for others, being a good listener, and being a rock others can depend on. As we mature in love we see what others experience as reality, and it becomes part of the context of our communication with them. This is all done on the intuitive level. Our gentleness, the way we treat others, is our gift to life.

The way that God translates through my experience is an extreme devotion to realize Him. Any thought that arises is not accepted at face value. It is looked at and inspected, or simply eschewed. What does this thought mean? What does this say about me? This is all done on a silent, intuitive level, closer to feeling than thinking.

What is found limiting or an error in my experience, I find myself saying something like, "I don't know anything Lord. Help me see." This clears the mind from attachment to one's own ignorance and gives an empty canvas to work from. I simply acknowledge my limitation and lay it before Him. Then I let Him do the rest.

CHAPTER 15
SUCCESS

Humble yourselves before the Lord
and He will exalt you.[68]

Part 1

It appears the motive behind human action is essentially a ploy to feel complete. We are constantly trying to choose for that which will complete us in that moment. However, when we look honestly at this dance, it never happens. But the person just continues on with this belief gnawing at them, bidding them to keep trying. It's plain to see, a person doesn't know how to be complete on their own.

The successful people in this world are attracted to that which brings about the most advantageous outcome in the long term. The other end of the spectrum is the person who has no energy to

---

[68] James 4:10

choose anything other than an attempt at immediate pleasure. There is little to no thought of consequences for them. The successful are very aware that each and every thing one does has consequences. Most of us bargain with choices ranging between immediate gratification and long-term security.

I decided to add this chapter while nearly finished with this book. In truth, this chapter could have been a book by itself. There is so much to say about this topic. However, I have written what I feel is the most accessible, essential, and beneficial to the reader interested in this topic. It seems to me that there are many who may resonate with this chapter, entitled "Success".

While most people are trying to get ahead in life and are driven by ideas of success, they might think, "what does loving without conditions have to do with me? How would this benefit me or help me meet my desired ends?" I will be upfront. It may not help you meet your desired ends. That is because your desired ends may be too narrow and small. You're shooting at the wrong bullseye. This path will expand your horizons and help you achieve more than you ever thought possible, surpassing your previous plans.

The path of loving without conditions eschews the short-lived, short-sighted, temporary, immediate pleasure and short-term gains for greater returns, more security, more fulfillment, more happiness, more freedom and better outcomes in the short and long-term. By aligning with the path of *loving without conditions*, we automatically orient towards that which brings long-term success. This path turns out to be the best investment for our precious life energy. We find that the more loving we are, the more energy there is available to us. Limiting emotions are healed and their stranglehold tends to dissipate and even disappear forever. We feel freer. The mind becomes more clear. The options available to us are more vast and optimal. We intuitively know how to handle what used to confuse us. One soon finds that life interacts with us differently.

The "lucky break" doesn't exist. The eyes of love reveal that everything is connected and alive. There is nothing in this universe that is accidental or separate from the whole. Nothing is "got away with". Everything is in perfect order. To the mind? No. To the Laws of God? Yes. Therefore, loving without conditions enhances all levels of our life and blesses those around us… even for all time. It is therefore the ultimate path of success in life.

Most of the world has a short-sighted vision of what success is, and normally this boils down to (a.) social approval and (b.) monetary gain. If extreme monetary gain is the goal of your life, I can tell you the simple formula to achieve this: go work your butt off. Get moving! Focus your life energy on that which brings about monetary reward. Make shrewd decisions, and you will likely prosper. However, my understanding is that you'll soon find that this fruit is limited. There will be an ache inside, a longing for something… call it "home". We soon find we would rather be whole, complete, secure, and at peace inside than to only experience fickle approval and worldly success. In my own observation, I will say for most people, we aren't actually ready for inner peace. We say we want it, but we want it from our own devices and terms. In other words, we want life to be a certain way that we see it because we are so sure that "then we'll be happy". We have a concept of how it "should" be. However, as many have found, this is a never-ending loop of dissatisfaction.

When our dream of success is fulfilled, we can become disillusioned by who we thought we were and what life was. It never did fulfill us. This is a breaking point for many.

When I was in college, I was going through changes. During the first semester of my senior year, my then girlfriend and I were crowned homecoming king and queen. The moment the crown was placed upon my head, I went through a transformation that is hard to describe.

At that precise moment, I realized that success to me had essentially been about getting approval from the world, that was my inner motive or drive. I had subtly held the thought that this was going to make me happy. Suddenly, I saw that it was hollow and an illusion. A solid underpinning of my personality had died... in a millisecond. I looked over at my girlfriend and thought, "Who are you? Who am I? What is this?" The accompanying feeling was timeless, so I can feel it now as I write. There was a transcendent feeling of freedom, but also followed by confusion and disorientation. When I walked off the stage, I was a different person. I had seen through the dangling carrot of approval that I had been seeking.

Through surrendering to Christ, one discovers true abundance. It reveals that God is in our favor. Life is designed perfectly for our growth. As we grow and expand so does our experience of life and God. We are never alone or unaided. God is power. In bringing the spirit of Christ with us in all we do, we bring the power of God. That is why the miraculous is common for those that surrender to God.

Christ knew that life reflects our inner relationship with God. Through this relationship, happiness and fulfillment will become a constant, since a person is pursuing the source of happiness directly. This can take some work in the beginning. However, the work pays off quickly. The experience of life gets better and better and becomes meaning itself.

Our experience is molded back to us by what we already hold to be true about life. Just like on Youtube, what pops up in our feed is what we've already invested in. If we think people are stingy, this will dominate our experience of others and be what we receive. If we think people are beautiful and giving, innocent by nature, that is what we will find. Life is the utmost of intelligence, it simultaneously reflects billions of people's mode of being back to them. Our life is known by its fruit. By entering upon and dedicating oneself to the path of Christ, our life becomes a healing balm to a disenfranchised people. What can bring greater joy and fulfillment than becoming a living sacrifice for others? We become a living sacrifice by giving up our judgements, our littleness, and our selfishness, and we ask that God be our light and strength. All glory be to God!

One does not necessarily have to change anything about their life and vocation for embarking on this path. However, one's life does become much simpler in the process. We are inspired and devoted to being a channel of peace above all else. It's akin to holding an intention while living one's everyday life. We become energized by love, by an all-encompassing and benevolent spirit. We ask for direction. In this process, our life develops deep meaning and purpose with all we do. Life becomes truly alive! It is not possible to verbally explain all that transpires... Suffice to say, it is a wonder.

As I look back on my life, I'm amazed and cannot wrap my mind around all the love, beauty, and miracles that have been bestowed upon my path. But I look back with fondness and gratitude. I am grateful for the constant feeling of inspiration.

It is love that supports life, and love that makes us a better employee, employer, parent, child, sibling, or citizen. With the intention to love without conditions, we can be said to be *living for heaven*. The fruits of such an intention are beyond this world, yet a part of it. "Be a light", Jesus said. This dedication is literally that.

Following the path of love, and refining that love, leads to the experience of joy. Living in a space of joy makes the idea of seeking happiness from the world irrelevant. The source of happiness has always been within us. Joy becomes the "modus operandi". Gone is the need to seek out pleasure; one is consciously experiencing the wellspring of happiness as a way of being. Going on a trip to Mexico, for example, isn't really all that attractive to me. I think most would see such a trip as a temporary break and escape from "the grind". What do I have to escape from or take a break from? My life is vacation. Jesus says "My yoke is easy and my burden is light".[69] This is true whether I work a few hours or 65 hours a week. I can go on a vacation and be complete and happy. In fact, I would if I was asked to go by a loved one. However, I don't seek it out. Why would I? Joy is in being! When one does go on vacations, one also enjoys them to their fullest. But the objective doesn't change. God is, and I am here to know Him... the ultimate relationship. The most fulfilling relationship. This could be said to be the ultimate point of existence. It is the relationship that is beyond time so as to be everlasting. With the love that I feel from this relationship, I'm inspired to be what I am to the world to the fullest. What I am to this world I cannot say, I can only be. We come to know abundance itself. The miraculous, the beautiful, the lovely... is 'what is'. It could be no other way.

The primary cause of our unhappiness is ignorance. We don't know what leads to true happiness, as we are clouded by our ignorance. In our ignorance, we grow attached to that which degrades truth. We say, "Well, that's who I am." And we accept less than love as reality. Our lifestyle patterns don't align with knowing truth, they often align with escape and frailty. "Being",

---

[69] Matthew 11:29

as a separate individual, is a hard burden to bear. This path allows for the forbearance of that burden.

It takes tremendous courage to be willing to surrender to God in a world of unpredictability. We are constantly being tugged on by a need to feel secure. Although we eventually find that life is only chaotic on the surface. The unstable part is the mental/emotional clutter that we carry. When this level of being is brought into order, we are ripe to discover the greater depths of knowledge about life. Namely, that it is beautiful. In order to know this magnificence, we have to be willing to let go of our attachments to the un-magnificent, ie., the patterns of escape and ignorance embedded in our being. We need to be able to see that the mind is not the savior of mankind. The mind divides life; however, when coupled with Spirit, it is brought into order. Without owning one's spiritual reality, mankind is lost.

We often want to hold onto things less than love simply because they are familiar. We identify with them. It just feels easier. As creatures of habit with a drive to "feel safe", we cowardly hide behind our conformed patterns and won't challenge these patterns because we don't know what's on the other side of them. A fruit of this path is that it helps us remove the patterns that have limited us since birth. We are inspired with devotion by the Holy Spirit for change for the better.

Instead of learning a particular technique for change in a given part of our lives, as we find in the Self Help sections of book stores, we are spearheading change directly where it matters most: in the heart of our being. We become more self-aware. We analyze our thoughts and behaviors more often. This puts the mind's thought and behavioral patterns under scrutiny. The mind's thought patterns are confronted for the repetitious programs that they are. Holding the mind accountable leads to a freer existence, as it is through the mind that we experience life. From this scrutiny and self-reflection comes a deeper understanding, without which we cannot readily grow and change for the better.

True success is having no lack. This book is being written from "no lack". It is written from abundance. This author has no desire for gain from this writing. It comes from the purity of the love of his relationship with the Divine. It comes from inspiration. It is an outpouring. I am complete if people read this. I am also complete if people do not read this. I am being what I am, and that is enough. All my needs are fulfilled. And if the body gets sick and dies today, that is ok too. I was what I am and that is enough.

The only place of "no lack" is to be in the security and abundance of the Love of God. Many are the worldly thinkers that talk "about" peace. This is ultimately a fool's errand because there is no peace in the world of form. If you don't have it now, you don't have it to share with others.

Few are those that have taken the leap into *being*. The leap that expands one's horizons precipitously... even unimaginably. Your journey towards success will not be complete until there is no lack. The only place this is found, by one means or another, is through the act of surrendering to one's Source. That's what this book is ultimately about. Knowing Source and knowing success are not distinct. We often project a specialness on particular forms of success in the world, but are they success at all? The grass only appears greener from within the realm of chaos and ignorance. It is not. The truth is that true success is open and available to everyone right this instant. It is always available. You be it.

By putting into action the intention of unconditional love, one can change and grow rapidly. In doing so, one begins to shine with the qualities that we all admire. In general, we can say at least some of those qualities are: being dependable, calm, energetic, compassionate, calm, welcoming, courageous, understanding, intelligent, lighthearted, patient, fun, loyal, loving, joyful, giving, responsible, caring, affirming, uplifting, and forgiving. Any rational employer would obviously jump at a chance to hire someone with these qualities. If you're an entrepreneur, it is more than likely that others will seek you out to do business with you; they will want to help make you successful.

When we compete with others, we can compete to our greatest ability through this path. It's not out of spite, but out of love for the game. We even love our opponents. This brings out the best in others. We enhance each other. You are aligned with the highest good for all. The overall experience of the sport becomes elevated. This is freedom.

We can become a beacon of freedom in business that wins by alignment with Power (Laws of Divinity, Freedom, Love). This powerful mode of being reorganizes everything around it. It sets a bar of excellence. Operating in this manner is a light shining from a hill for others to see. There are so few who operate in this realm of heart in business, while so many are operating from the desire of gain. Those that do succeed in ways unimaginable. Our business becomes an extension of our joy, and our work becomes a blessing. We love our work. We love our life. We become the most sought after in our field.

Having grown up with a love for basketball, I was pulled back into watching NBA basketball because of Stephen Curry. He shines with a selfless brilliance in my opinion. It appeared to me that he was aligned with Power as he played. There is a freedom about the way he plays on court. Even though he was short for NBA standards, he was doing things we had never seen before, even altering the game for everyone that plays.

Steph uplifts the players around him, helping his team play with joy. This is part of the engine, along with selfless ball movement, that his team uses while dominating opponents. All the players are working together in a kind of harmony and unison. You can see their smiles radiating and watch the team go into a near "flow state" together, which, when entered, they become invincible.

Kobe Bryant came to know this space as well. He understands Stephen and was able to define what it means to play with fearless surrender in the space of joy. In an interview, Kobe had this to say about Stephen:

I see a calmness about him. I think it's something a lot of [people] don't understand. There's a serious calmness about him which is extremely deadly. Because he's not up, he's not down. He's not contemplating what just happened before, or worrying about what happens next. He's just there. When a player has the skills and has trained himself... and then you mix that with this calmness and poise, then you have a serious problem on your hands. So when I watch him play... that's what I see.[70]

When I find myself watching the expression of grace in sports, I will often break down in tears and feel ecstatic. That is common for any outlet where love is expressed, whether it be art, athletics, public speeches or simply a gaze from a passerby.

Upon taking a break from writing a moment ago, I watched highlights of a woman's basketball guard. Tears erupted as I watched her shoot the ball effortlessly from extremely long distances. I witnessed an economy in her play, nothing was wasted. Her space of flow was apparent. This spiritual space comes as a gift.

Even the atheist is unknowingly attracted to the qualities of God expressed through their fellow human beings. They might be disagreeable to the packaging or its labels, but not to the fruit. That is why becoming Christ's teaching is important: *it speaks*

---

[70] Via Espn 12/23/15 https://www.youtube.com/watch?v=r-06h4mSRc0

unendingly. It doesn't force anyone or anything. It just is. It radiates power and life responds accordingly. When we love we are with God, an expression of power just by being.

God is open, free and available. To be loving is to bring God into all we do. It is the ultimate coming home because we feel complete and secure. To be in the Presence of God is to be free of needs or wants, yet unlimited in potential.[71] The surrendered servant of God has a powerful effect on this world and alters it forever.

Part 2

You may be at the beginning of your path in Loving Without Conditions. This path is realizable and achievable in this life for you. Christ would not have commanded it if it was not. It starts as an intention and then turns into a way of being. I wanted to offer a few simple steps to apply to your life to help get you started. Success on this journey is success in all you do. They cannot be separated.

1.) *Decide to do the little things well* (the small, simple tasks). This will bring confidence and fluidity to your life. It will also help bring clarity and order, which is needed to be productive and successful in the world.

2.) *Be in the practice of turning to God nonverbally with a simple "here I am Lord" (the benefit of this practice is beyond words).*

---

[71] John 4:32

The simple act of turning to God kindles the flame of love in your relationship with your Creator. Bringing this relationship into one's day is the wellspring from where we experience "flow" and beauty. We drop egocentric thinking and open up to patterns of greatness and higher modes of being.

3.) *Decide that God loves you and already knows all potential good and bad about you.* We can't hide. So why try? Everything about us is already known. Every hair on your head is counted. And still, there is no judgment upon you by your Creator. There is complete acceptance of you. Accept this and live.

4.) *Accept that God made you just as you are, both the pluses and minuses were inherent in you the moment you came to be.* Knowing this, decide to love yourself exactly as you are right now. In loving yourself as you are, one has greater freedom and opportunity to change and grow when necessary.

5.) *Decide to laugh at all negative and judgmental thoughts.* They are not you. Turn to God instead. To laugh at them is to be detached. Hating them is to be in bondage to them.

6.) *Dance a lot.* Every chance you get. You cannot apply this and not be uplifted into heaven. Dance in joy, and life will reveal her melody.

7.) *All you can ever experience is what you give to life.* In other words, give away your beauty so that you may know beauty. This helps reveal your unimaginable truth.

8.) *Accept that your finances will always be ok.* That all life is already taken care of. These are the words of the Master.

Listen, obey, and act accordingly. He taught the laws of freedom. Problems arise when we get in His way.

9.) *Hold in mind a positive resolution for all relationships and dealings.* What you hold in mind tends to happen. That resolution can be as simple as, "whatever happens will benefit everyone. God's will be done."

10.)*If you haven't cried this week, then release what is binding your heart.* There is so much beauty to behold. Tears for beauty and compassion are what heals this world of suffering from the inside out. Let your light so shine before men!

Most people judge the idea of success from temporary achievements in time. That is because they cannot see beyond the short term and temporary. A child wants the candy and pouts when she is unable to have it. The child doesn't see that being respectful, cooperative, and patient achieves more candy for them in the long term. It is this way with success in life.

One might look sweet in an Instagram photo. The world may be mesmerized by its charm. We might be envious of the person in the photo. The wise, however, don't read into appearances. Does the photo reflect the success of being or just a short-lived appearance of power? Are they loyal, generous, respectful, honest, forthright, understanding, intelligent, patient, balanced, and driven? Those are the qualities that make for long-term success. Appearances are misleading. Don't play the appearances game.

If you want true long-term success, align with the qualities of love. One will then automatically empower the qualities of success. The more an enterprise embodies the elements of Christ, the greater the chances that the business will experience long-term success.

The Self Help section of a bookstore has hundreds upon hundreds of books about achieving success. Many of those books highlight a certain concept to supposedly help the reader succeed. I was shocked when I realized what the authors were doing. Knowingly or unknowingly, they were cherry-picking a specific quality of those aligned with power and reflecting that one quality as an avenue to success. However, their mistake is that they fail to see that success isn't real until it becomes a way of being.

When you align with this path you don't have to try to be a success, you become those qualities by default. The advantages of the unconditionally loving are numerous. In business, having a keen intuition is a tremendous gift. Things will get done faster. Options are weeded through more rapidly. People are seen for their essence. Bad ideas are seen more rapidly, which can save a business an unnecessary expenditure of energy. The "good break" tends to come to those with an abundance of goodwill.

When we look at the news, we will often see businesses falling because of the shortsightedness of their management. Many businesses are corrupted from within and cannot recover from sexual assault, embezzlement, or from the trap of greed. When a person gets put in power, they can easily lose their foundation and fall prey to the appearance of success without actually becoming it. One can feel special. One can also take advantage of a position of power.

On this path we are dealing with the shortcomings of ego from the start. That way, should worldly power come our way, we'll be prepared for the responsibility. The successful do in fact feel a responsibility to be what they are to the fullest and to share that with the world. Our success glorifies both God and man.

CHAPTER 16
CONCLUSION

Be perfect, therefore, as your Heavenly Father
is perfect.[72]

This book was written from personal experience from a few decades of dedication to this path. I would not write this book if I did not feel adequately familiar with the topic. This world has enough people and experts that know "about". It's time we become experts that know "from". There is a big difference between the two. One is on the conceptual level and the other is on the practical and experiential.

It is time for our preachers, pastors, spiritual leaders and teachers to seek first the Kingdom of Heaven. To leave behind worldly pursuits. We are to be preparing people for eternity! This is an important job.

---

[72] Matthew 5:48

I'm tired of reading the headlines and seeing another scandal associated with the name of God. "If they only knew how sweet the fruit of the Kingdom they represent," I've often thought. We have to be prepared for ushering in the spirit of wisdom, truth, and love. We affect every living being through our life. It doesn't matter if you have direct contact with others or not, you matter simply by the fact of existing. You and I know each other on some level already. That awareness might be dormant, but once awake, you will never want to go back. *Come home, come home... ye who are weary come home...*

The want and will to love without conditions is a response to God's grace in your life. It's a true sign that the Holy Spirit is in your life. Align your life with God. Ask God directly, "Lord, make me a channel of Thy peace... How would You have me?" This path is no joke. It is yours for the taking. The angels in heaven rejoice at the prospect of you joining hands with them. This is the covenant of love. This life will be over fast for you. What do you want to be remembered for when you are sitting on your death bed? You will never regret surrendering your life to the Source of Love.

The more spiritually advanced we are here on earth, the more we take responsibility for our life experiences, the more grace and goodness will be in our life. Through this process, we carve out heaven here on earth. We become a living sacrifice. We open the gates to grace.

A note to those of a different religious or spiritual belief system: Loving Christ does not go against your nature. It is obviously a wise choice to align with this Divine being of love. Christ doesn't care if you subscribe to the Christian religion. All religion is made by human beings and is in fact limited. There are obvious faults in all takes on religion. Connect with Him in your heart. He's big enough to meet you where you are at. Leave all else behind. He loves you where you are. He came to liberate. Not incarcerate.

If you follow this path, you will find Him in the way that is your delight. He is waiting for you. You will know Him by the freedom and beauty that comes to your life. You lose nothing. You gain everything. It's ok to consider Him a friend or a guide. His Spirit is already upon you. It only awaits your approval.

Do you have to be devoted to Christ to be devoted to loving without conditions? Of course not! But if the path is followed devotedly, I believe the dilemma of what Christ is will be solved along the way. There are no arguments on this path. All becomes clear.

Seek God first and He will direct your path.

The problems of this world will not be solved at the mental level. Science is useful, but it is not a savior to humankind. Politics are useful, but they aren't the savior to humankind. The world has already been saved. The way has been shown. Find a way to know this.

You have gifts. Some you have already come to know. Some have yet to be discovered. All these gifts will become magnified by this path. In the time of Jesus, and shortly thereafter, there were all kinds of miracles. People had genuine and pronounced spiritual gifts.

I presume that at some point the politics within the church, which come from the mind of humans, held more weight than did the simple and practical, namely surrendering to Jesus. Because of this, we stopped readily having spiritual gifts.

If there is one thing my life has shown me, it is that God wants to gift us. He wants to work through us. Spiritual gifts are not something to seek directly, because we should seek to conform to the Spirit of Christ so that these gifts have meaning and efficacy. I believe that spiritual gifts are something that can happen more readily on this path than people are accustomed. It's time for spiritual maturity, in the name of Jesus, to be a focus for Christians. That open, loving, wise, accepting, and strong way of being. It's time to be authorities on spiritual matters because we live *by* the Spirit. It's time to let the Word of Truth live in our hearts.

But a time is coming and has now come when the true worshipers will worship the Father in spirit and in truth, for the Father is seeking such as these to worship Him.
God is spirit, and his worshipers must worship in the Spirit and in truth. "

(John 4:23-24 NIV)

There is much chaos in our world. It always has been this way it seems and likely always will. Even when there are times without war, there are still natural disasters, sickness and famine. It is difficult for a single human to be at peace with themselves, let alone with 7 billion others.

There is a yearning inside of us to get back to the garden, to be in peace. A map was given to us through Jesus Christ. It seems quite clear he didn't speak it just to give it lip service. Did this path lose value to us as Christians? We can speak of a second coming, and hope for it all day, but who is in control of that? Not us. Then how are we to bring Christ back to earth? That answer is staring at us in the face: through us. A second coming happens every time we say "yes" to the Spirit of Christ. That all-encompassing love that unites us all. We cannot give in to apathy as Christians. We must do the work as Christ asks. Progress, not perfection.

If there is in fact a second coming, and there may be in your lifetime, you must be ready. How are you to be ready? Well, isn't it obvious? Follow the teaching of Christ! He cannot come where he is not welcomed.

I felt a calling and spiritual awakening in my college years. Looking back at my younger years, it seems like I was asleep. I see that I was clouded by emotion and bogged down with a low level depression. My thinking was not clear. My life energy was lacking.

In college, I suddenly had the ability to think more succinctly and clearly. I was pulling from a completely different strata of thought. I suddenly had charisma. I could look into the hearts of others. Out of the blue, I could write songs. In one sitting I could effortlessly write two songs. I once sat down in a cafe and wrote 5 children's books in a row. The ability to heal came. The ability to see things in the future has come. There's an unspoken communication with everything. Times of raw emotion with tears will arise, for the joy and love of existence. All these things were nascent earlier in life. I was transformed and felt an inner calling to perfect my love for God for a greater purpose.

My grades all shot up in college. I had the ability to pay better attention and offer better ideas. My life enjoyment sky-rocketed as well. Loving people made college an amazing experience. If you knew what kind of a student I was in high school, you'd have been hard-pressed to believe that I would be writing a book such as this. This didn't seem part of the trajectory whatsoever, not even on the radar.

If you ask me what you'll get out of this journey, I can only say much more than you had bargained for. It's true, patience is necessary, along with steadfastness. When you call upon God to align you with His Truth, certain things must come into play. Some things take a little time to orchestrate; however, something will be set in motion for you. You will never be the same.

I think I was fortunate to go through such a transformation so readily. It felt like I understood what was happening on an intuitive level, yet at the same time I have never really met anyone who went through that strong and rapid of a shift in being. At least no one prior had revealed such things. However, I later read about near-death experience survivors like Howard Storm and Betty J. Eadie, and I could relate to their transformative experiences in my own way. I went through such a drastic change that I couldn't speak about it with my family. I didn't know where to begin. Everything shifted for me, and I still don't know how to be "normal". I frequently have to remind myself how others think and what their motives are. I have learned to be small and quiet... a better listener. At my five-year college reunion, I stood out as "weird", I was told. For years, even though I tried not to, I couldn't hide my inspiration on social media. It wasn't until I started writing this book that I could stop exclaiming about the love of God on Facebook. I guess I needed an outlet.

Not everyone will go through a change that drastic. Even though my orientation shifted rapidly, I still had to go back and face my backlog of emotional injuries and nuances. In the beginning, I had hoped they might just go away on their own. Eventually, I realized that what we don't face controls us on subtle levels. It felt freeing to finally humble myself and own myself at the emotional level. There's a security and enjoyment that one can only have when one has healed the pricks of emotional upheaval held within.

I want to highly recommend that if you are at a standstill in your walk with God, that you ask him directly: "What's holding me back Lord? Where are there limitations on my love?" If you're not feeling amazingly joyful and free, there is more ground to cover on your journey. You'll go until God takes the reins. I call that *the surrendered state.*

This journey will allow you to understand yourself in great depth. This will obviously help you know others with amazing depth as well. For truly, in growing spiritually, we find out that everything that lies inside us is essentially what lies inside most all of us. This helps us carry the utmost compassion for the human experience. Other will turn to us for healing, to be heard, understood, and seen.

This path is essentially asking God to be a servant. He will gift you with the tools to do so. Treat them with humble respect. If God doesn't give you any outward gifts, accept that it's for your own good. Sometimes gifts are held back because they would not benefit the person or are unnecessary. Sometimes gifts arrive as needed. The thing to be most grateful for is that we walk with love and grace.

Dedicate every day to serving the Lord. What might seem like a chore to the mind at first ends up being the utmost in satisfaction and joy. You were made to shine like the sun. Keep in mind:

where there is humility, there is God. Without humility, there is no God in your experience.

Are you ready to take this journey? This is the prayer I've said for the last twenty years. Please say it with me if you feel like making it yours too: *Lord, please make me a channel of Thy peace... how would you have me Lord? I'm ready to do Thy bidding. Do with me according to Thy will.*

That's it. God will do the rest. We need only say "yes" each day and reaffirm our dedication to our Beloved. I will see you there, at the foot of the cross.

ENDNOTE

Thank you for taking the time to read this book. May you be blessed with the love that lives through our Lord Jesus Christ and surrounds you now. Amen!

ABOUT THE AUTHOR

Born and raised in Southern Minnesota, Ben graduated from Gustavus Adolphus College and afterwards spent a summer as a wilderness guide on Lake Superior. Contemplating the Bible with others in nature initiated a desire to know Christ more deeply, even becoming single-minded in seeking Him.

What's unique about this work is that it is not coming from any kind of religious education or formality. It's coming from the seeker's heart of wanting to know Christ through pursuing Him directly.

Ben currently lives in St. Paul, MN, where he has led groups on exploring this path. His last few decades have been devoted to love and surrender through Christ. What is written in this book is the fruit of this journey. May it be pleasing in His sight.

Ben is an Unconditional Love Mentor, Surrender Coach and Motivational Speaker.

Email: benbigelowauthor@outlook.com

May God bless you and keep you,
make his face shine upon you
and grant you peace.